WHAT THEY DON'T TEACH YOU
IN LIBRARY SCHOOL

ALA GUIDES FOR THE BUSY LIBRARIAN

WHAT THEY DON'T TEACH YOU
IN LIBRARY SCHOOL

ELISABETH DOUCETT

AMERICAN LIBRARY ASSOCIATION
CHICAGO   2011

Elisabeth Doucett is director of the Curtis Memorial Library in Brunswick, Maine. She holds an MLS from Simmons College, where she was elected to the Beta Phi Mu Honor Society, and an MBA in marketing from the J. L. Kellogg School of Management at Northwestern University. She is the author of *Creating Your Library Brand*. Her strategy and marketing proficiencies were developed during more than a decade spent in the consumer packaged goods industry as a marketing director at Quaker Oats and Dunkin' Donuts and as a brand manager at Kraft Foods in the Maxwell House Coffee division.

ALA Editions purchases fund advocacy, awareness, and accreditation programs for library professionals worldwide.

ISBN: 978-0-8389-3592-7

Printed in the United States of America
15 14 13 12 11   5 4 3 2 1

While extensive effort has gone into ensuring the reliability of the information appearing in this book, the publisher makes no warranty, express or implied, with respect to the material contained herein.

Library of Congress Cataloging-in-Publication Data
Doucett, Elisabeth.
  What they don't teach you in library school / Elisabeth Doucett.
    p. cm. -- (ALA guides for the busy librarian)
  Includes bibliographical references and index.
  ISBN 978-0-8389-3592-7 (alk. paper)
  1. Library science. 2. Library science--Vocational guidance. I. Title.
  Z665.D685 2011
  020.23--dc22

                                                              2010013642

Book design in Charis SIL and Soho Gothic Pro by Casey Bayer.

⊚ This paper meets the requirements of ANSI/NISO Z39.48-1992 (Permanence of Paper).

ALA Editions also publishes its books in a variety of electronic formats. For more information, visit the ALA Store at www.alastore.ala.org and select eEditions.

CONTENTS

INTRODUCTION

I went to graduate school to get my master's in library science when I was in my forties. As I progressed through the library science program, graduated, looked for my first job in the profession, and then started working, I discovered gaps in my library training at each step that I wish had been covered by classes while I was at school. I got lucky in some cases because my earlier career in business had taught me some important skills that helped bridge those gaps. However, in other situations (such as what to do with a library patron on drugs or how to deal with a leaky roof) I was completely unprepared. I kept thinking there should be a class that teaches all those disparate skills, but I've never seen one in any MLS curriculum.

As a result, after writing my first book (*Creating Your Library Brand*) I decided that my next book would be the class that taught those things we never learned in library school. This was a bit of a tough sell, because the topics that fit into "what I never learned at library school, but wish I had" are so wide and varied. To manage this issue, I decided to break the book into the following parts: (1) the skills that would be helpful to have as you prepare to graduate with your new master's degree, (2) the skills that would be helpful as you begin your first job as a librarian, and (3) the skills that would be helpful after you've gotten a little experience on the job.

My goal for this book is to provide some very basic, down-to-earth help and training that will help the reader move smoothly into a new profession and be successful. I would like to think of this book as a way of mentoring those individuals new to librarianship. None of these chapters are meant to be academic in nature. They aren't detailed and they aren't exhaustive. Instead, the chapters are more in the form of an informal conversation (much like what you might have with a mentor), designed to give you enough information to "get by," and written in a simple format that can be easily and quickly read and understood. Each chapter can be read on its own and has a short list of additional resources that should be helpful if you want to dive deeper into the topic. Good luck, and I wish you much success in your job as a librarian.

PART I | HELPFUL TO KNOW BEFORE YOU GET YOUR FIRST JOB AS A LIBRARIAN

ONE | THE RIGHT JOB

WHAT THIS CHAPTER IS ABOUT

Providing you with a methodology to figure out if a job offer is the right one for you

WHY SHOULD YOU CARE?

This one should be obvious. It wouldn't make much sense to put all that time and energy and money into going to graduate school, and then end up in a job you hate.

THE HEART OF THE MATTER

After you graduate with your newly minted master's in library science, it's very likely that your first overwhelming urge will be to *find a job*. There are very few students who get away from graduate school debt-free. Therefore, on top of the natural desire to get going and put to work all that great information you've learned, there is also the more practical consideration of addressing the accumulated debts hanging over your head. Because of these pressures and a lack of experience in job hunting among many library school grads, new librarians frequently take the first job they are offered, regardless of the pay, the environment, or the responsibilities that they will be assuming. As a result, often individuals leave their first job as librarians within one or two years because they didn't understand and weren't ready for their job situation. This chapter is meant to give you a simple process to follow to help you determine if a job you are offered is (a) a good job, and (b) a good job for you (sometimes two very different things).

Step 1: *Before you even start interviewing for jobs, take an honest look at your financial situation and develop a clear understanding of your monthly expenses.* What does this have to do with a job? If you don't know how much you spend every month, how will you know how much you must earn to cover those expenses? Be very detailed in your budget; if you have to guess, guess high rather than low. If you don't know how much you spend on one of these budget items (frequently people aren't aware of how much they spend on food), track your expenses in that category for a month by writing down every penny you spend. Do yourself a favor here—don't *estimate* what you spend. Make sure you *know* what you spend. It will make a world of difference in helping you develop a lifestyle that you can enjoy. If you really want to do this right,

Understanding Your Monthly Expenses

You need to make sure your budget is inclusive of all your expenses. The following is a list of possible budget expenses to consider. Generally, it is easiest if you identify these expenses on a monthly basis:

Mortgage or rent	Medical expenses/medical insurance
Utilities (gas, electric, cable TV, Internet)	Dental
Food	House/apartment insurance
Car payments	Credit card payments
Car insurance	Student loan payments
Gas for car	Savings
Other transportation expenses	Pet expenses
Clothing	Entertainment/fun
Telephone	Gym membership

buy simple budget-tracking software such as Quicken or Microsoft Money. You will be able to download your bank statement directly into the software, and it will track your expenses for you. It's a great investment and one that I highly recommend, particularly for people in professions like librarianship in which no one ever makes an excess of money.

Once you have your monthly budget figured out, multiply it by twelve. This is the minimum amount of money that you must make in your job each year to cover your expenses. This is your first criterion for deciding if a job is a good one for you. Obviously, if a job doesn't pay enough to cover your expenses, it probably isn't a great option for you. Either that, or you will need to figure out what you can cut out of your monthly expenses to live within your salary.

When you are looking at this first criterion, make sure that you aren't making a common mistake: the amount of money that your library offers as a salary is not the amount of money you will take home every year. The amount that your employer offers to pay you per year is your *gross* pay, or the amount of salary that you make before taxes and benefit expenses such as health insurance and contributions to a retirement account are deducted. These costs will substantially reduce the actual cash that you take home. Once your benefit expenses are deducted from your gross salary, you will have your *net* pay—the actual cash that goes home with you. How can you figure your net versus gross pay when evaluating a job? Table 1 shows a simple calculation you can use. You can also find net pay calculators online to help you do the same, or check out www.ehow.com or www.ask.com for instructional articles.

Step 2: *Trust your gut instincts.* Life is looking good. You sent a résumé to a library for a job that you know will pay enough to cover your expenses, and you got an interview. You go to the library for a day of interviewing. At the end of the day, you shake hands and head home. You walk in the door of your home, take off your shoes, and head to the refrigerator. This is when you should stop everything. Take a deep breath, sit down in a comfortable chair, and spend ten minutes listening to yourself. That means you don't talk to anyone, you don't watch the television, you don't phone anyone or imme-diately text six friends about your interview. You just listen to the feelings in your gut. What are your feelings telling you? Are you excited and energized by your day? Are you thinking, "Oh my gosh, it would be fabulous to work in that library!" Do you feel happy and hopeful? If so, life is good and you can go to step three. If not, stop for a minute (again). You have to listen to your instincts when it comes to job hunting (and finding a life partner and buying a house and just about anything else!).

Table 1
Example of How to Calculate Your Net (Take-Home) Pay

Step	Action	Calculation	Example
1	Determine your proposed gross pay	What does this job pay per year as defined by your potential employer?	Gross pay = $40,000 per year
2	Determine how much you would have to pay for medical and dental insurance. After you get a job offer, ask your potential employer for this information, since it will differ substantially from employer to employer.	Subtract the cost of medical insurance and dental insurance.	Subtract dental/medical expenses = $200 per month or $2,400 per year = $37,600
3	Determine your Social Security tax (FICA) deduction	Calculate your FICA by multiplying your net pay minus your medical and dental coverage by .062.	FICA expense = $37,600 x .062 = $2,331 $37,600 - $2,331 = $35,269
4	Medicare tax	Calculate your Medicare tax by multiplying your net pay minus medical and dental coverage times .0145.	Medicare = $37,600 x .0145 = $545 $35,269 - $545 = $34,724
5	Retirement	Ask what is the maximum amount that you can contribute to your retirement account. Generally, it is a percentage of your gross pay. Let's assume it is 6%.	$34,724 x .06 = $2,083 $34,724 - $2,083 = $32,641

Step	Action	Calculation	Example
6	Federal tax	You will have to research the current federal tax rate, based on your salary. Go right to the source: www.irs.gov. Generally, if you are single and estimate making between $32,000 and $78,000 your federal tax rate will be 25%. Let's use that number, but keep in mind this does not include any deductions that you might apply. However, it will give you a general understanding of how much money will come out of your paycheck.	$32,641 x .25 = $8,160 $32,641 – $8,160 = $24,481
7	State tax	You will also have to research your current state tax rate. Two good sources are www .retirementliving.com and www.bankrate.com. Both provide state-by-state tax rate information. Let's use Maine's rate of 8.5%. Again, keep in mind this does not include any deductions you might be able to apply.	$32,641 x .085 = $2,774 $24,481 – $2,774 = $21,707
8	Net pay	This is approximately what you can expect to take home each year. Divide it by 12 and you can see how much you will have to spend each month. Looks a lot smaller than where we started, doesn't it?	$21,707 ÷ 12 = $1,809 per month

Here's a story to help you understand why you should trust your instincts. At one point in my career in business, I applied for a job that looked perfect on paper. It paid about thirty thousand dollars a year more than what I was currently making. It was a job with lots of budget and personnel responsibility, doing work that I knew and liked. But on the day that I was called with a job offer, I got off the telephone, sat down, and started to cry. Obviously, my gut instinct was telling me something was wrong. But I didn't listen. I took the job because it paid so well and my brain kept telling me it was the right thing to do. Less than two years later, I left that job, having been miserable for almost every minute I was there. My gut knew that I shouldn't have taken that job, but I talked myself into it. That almost never works out well. Listen to your instincts. If something seems wrong, then spend time to figure out what it is. Don't take a job because you *should* or because it looks like it must be perfect. Take the time to figure out how you feel—and then go to step three.

Step 3: *Now listen to your brain.* Despite everything I just wrote in step two, I do understand the realities of today's work environment. As I write this in fall of 2009, our country is in the worst economic situation it has been in for generations. Jobs are scarce, and people are struggling to pay their bills. You might say to me, "How can I be fussy about taking any job in this environment?" Let me be clear: I'm not telling you to pass on a job that doesn't feel right. Rather, I'm saying listen to your instincts and if something feels wrong for you, stop and take the time to figure out what the problem is. Once you know what this is, you can make a rational decision to accept a job even though you know there are issues. It is OK to walk into a job that is less than perfect, as long as your expectations are set accordingly and you plan to adjust your behavior to cope with those expectations. My mistake was thinking my new job was going to be perfect, and then struggling mightily when it wasn't. I had not developed any way of coping with the issues I faced in that job. If you go into a tough job prepared to cope with the issues at hand, the odds are very good that you will be successful. Basically this all boils down to one thought: be prepared. When you are prepared, you can generally manage any situation.

Step 4: *Do some more research.* The library world is a very small place, whether you choose to work in a public library, an academic library, or a special library. The odds are very good that if you ask one or several of your graduate school professors about the library at which you have been interviewing, they will be able to tell you (a) about the library's leadership, (b) about librarians from your school who have gone there, and (c) their opinions of the library as a first job opportunity for you. So take the time to ask. You are collecting information, and the informal feedback that you get from people with real experience with your potential employer will provide some of the most valuable input you can collect. Additionally, this type of information will help confirm or deny the initial impressions that you collected when you interviewed.

Also, don't forget to spend a lot of time on your potential employer's website. It will tell you a great deal about how the library presents itself to its public, how they think about information management, and how they spend money. All of these are very helpful data points for defining your perspective about this employer.

Step 5: *Make lists.* Sit down and write three lists, including a list of what you have to have, what you would like to have, and what you really couldn't care less about when it comes to a job. Be honest with yourself. If you've worked at other jobs, think about what made you happy and what made you miserable. If you've never had a job, think instead about what did and didn't work for you at school. Here are some questions to ask yourself as part of this process:

Do I need to have my own space at work, or am I comfortable sharing space? Some libraries have wonderful working spaces for staff. Other libraries have minimal or no space allocated to staff, or their staff areas are located in the most undesirable space in the library—usually the basement. When you are interviewing, ask to see the private workspace for staff so that you understand the situation you are getting into before you start.

Do I enjoy a very serious, purposeful environment, or am I happier with some fun built into the job? The environment of every library varies, usually depending a great deal on the attitude of the library director, who sets the tone of the workplace. If you are someone who wants to go to work and put all your energy and focus into your job, then don't accept a position where people are more relaxed and social interaction during the workday is considered the norm. How do you figure all this out in the course of interviewing? Staff workspaces provide great clues. If they are impersonal and one desk could be exchanged for another, then my guess would be that the focus is on the job. If you see very personalized desks with family pictures and plants and cartoons, then I would assume the environment is more social and relaxed.

Do I need or want a lot of supervision and teaching in my first job, or am I fairly comfortable figuring things out on my own? Some libraries have very detailed training programs for new employees. For library school graduates with less experience in the workplace, this can be particularly helpful because a training program can teach you much about formal skills and can also teach you the informal norms of the library. Norms are the unspoken expectations that you will find in any organization. Learning them can be exceptionally useful in helping you become an effective worker quickly.

Do I need positive feedback from my boss and coworkers, or do I provide my own positive feedback? This is an important question as you start to define what makes you happy. Some folks need to have the occasional "Good job!" or positive feedback from coworkers to feel like they are appreciated. Other people find their own satisfaction in a job well done and don't need positive input from others. If you have the first type of personality, don't go to a library with the second kind of environment. You'll never be happy in your job, because you will never feel appreciated.

Has the position been held by other people, and will I be expected to do the job exactly the same way they did? If so, am I OK with that? If not, am I comfortable with forging my own path? Some people are entrepreneurial by nature. By that I mean they enjoy working in a constantly changing, fluid environment, they like change, and they are comfortable with ambiguity. Other individuals want their job responsibilities to be more consistent, they like to understand how they fit into an environment, and they are comfortable doing repetitive elements of a job. By understanding which type of person you are, you'll have a better understanding of the type of library position you should seek out.

When I interviewed, did I like the people with whom I interviewed? This is one of those "listen to yourself" questions. I think it is important to like and enjoy the people with whom you work. You are around them seven to twelve hours a day, so to me it only makes sense to want to be around people whom you can enjoy.

When I interviewed was I myself, or was I being what I thought the employer wanted? I think this is a critical question to answer. Don't kid yourself on this one. No one can keep up a façade forever, so you might as well be yourself and understand that at some point you will find the right match for your capabilities.

All of these questions are guides to helping you determine the environment that makes you happiest. There are no right or wrong answers, just answers that either work for you or don't. Take a look at your potential new job and see how many of your "have to have's" are part of the job and how many aren't included. This will also start to give you some sense of whether this place will be a good fit for you.

Step 6: *Final review.* Finally, take the time to think carefully and reflect on all the information you've collected about this job. Does that data indicate that your gut instinct is right or wrong? Is your instinct meshing with the facts that you've collected, or is it contradicting what you've learned? If facts and feelings mesh, the odds are good that you have used both your instinct and your intellect to evaluate this job. The two agree that the job is either a good fit or a bad one—and in either case, you are probably correct, because you are considering the opportunity from a variety of ways.

If your instinct and your intellect disagree, here's what to do next. This will sound like something your mother would tell you to do, but it will help. (Mothers are actually pretty smart most of the time.) Take a sheet of paper, divide it into two columns, and write the pros of the job on one side and the cons on the other. Include both what you know and what you feel. If this job pays well and high salaries are important at this point in your life, write it down. If the other employees seem really depressed in their work and the whole library seems depressing, write that down. At the end, tally the pros and cons. Generally, you'll find one column clearly weighted over the other. However, the process and structure of writing everything out will actually be as helpful in clarifying the right decision for you.

Step 7: *Decision time.* Quick: if everything worked out perfectly, would you take this job or not? Don't stop to think any more, don't pause, and don't rationalize. Just ask yourself: do you want to work in this library or not?

The most important thing is that you have been very thoughtful in your decision making. Even if it isn't the perfect position for you and you decide to take it anyway, you are now walking in the door with a clear understanding of your environment. As a result you will be able to prepare accordingly and be confident about what you will be facing.

OTHER RESOURCES

Graham, Shawn. *Courting Your Career: Match Yourself with the Perfect Job.* Indianapolis, IN: JIST Works, 2008.
This guide uses dating as an analogy for finding the right match with a job. The information is easy to access and fun to read.

Monster.com. www.monster.com.
This is a commercial website for job seekers. However, it does offer some good articles providing advice about various aspects of job hunting and starting a new job.

Strayer, Susan D. *The Right Job, Right Now: The Complete Toolkit for Finding Your Perfect Career.* New York: St. Martin's Griffin, 2007.
This book has practical advice and ideas for every aspect of job hunting and finding the right match between you and your employer.

U.S. Bureau of Labor Statistics. "Evaluating a Job Offer." www.bls.gov/oco/oco20046.htm.
The U.S. Bureau of Labor Statistics' Online Occupational Outlook Handbook for 2010–2011 provides a good synopsis of what to consider when evaluating a job offer.

TWO | # PLANNING YOUR CAREER

WHAT THIS CHAPTER IS ABOUT

Putting together a career development plan for yourself and identifying low-cost resources for self-training

WHY SHOULD YOU CARE?

In today's economy many libraries are operating on a shoestring. Staff development funds are often the first things to be given up to budget reductions, and managers and administrators are so focused on meeting basic budget needs that they don't have the time or funds to concentrate on staff development and training. Therefore, the only person whom you can be absolutely sure will take care of your career and your training is you. You might ask why this is important if you just graduated from library school—do you really need to keep training? I've found training to be a lifelong pursuit. It is critical for two key reasons: it keeps you on top of changes in the profession (and the library profession is rapidly shifting right now), and lifelong learning increases your personal satisfaction in your career. It keeps you interested in the profession, it keeps you challenged in your responsibilities, and it ensures that you do well in your job.

This chapter is meant to provide some ideas about how you can begin building your own development plan as soon as you graduate from library school.

THE HEART OF THE MATTER

From your first day on your first job as a librarian, you should take ownership of your own career. That means that you should actively seek out and pursue opportunities for training and find the time to get the training. If your library can't afford to send you to seminars or training sessions, then find ways of getting that training on your own. But don't make the mistake of assuming that once you have received your master's in library science, you are done with your education. In fact, your education is only just beginning, and your worth as a librarian and your happiness in the profession will be in direct relationship to your ability to keep current with changes in the profession.

The following are some actions that need to be incorporated in your plans for your continuing education.

Specialize

If you want to build a reputation for yourself, it is helpful to have an area in which you specialize and can become an expert. This adds to your value in your library and helps make you a go-to person, rather than just another staff person. When I refer to specializations in this context, I don't mean topic specialization such as becoming an expert art history librarian. Rather, I'm talking about becoming an expert in some aspect of librarianship such as collection development, readers' advisory, library literacy training, or performance measurement.

Why is this a good thing? Because any time an issue comes up in your area of focus, you will be the official go-to person in your library. That makes you unique and valuable. Also, it gives you an area of interest on which to focus, which can make your job a lot more interesting over the long haul. For example, if you really enjoying talking to library users about books they might enjoy, then learning all the tools of readers' advisory will be fun and useful.

Before you decide to focus on learning more about a specific area of librarianship, spend some time thinking honestly about what you really enjoy. Do

Librarianship "Specialty" Areas to Consider Pursuing

Readers' Advisory

Helping readers find their next book

Collection Development

Planning and developing your library's collection of materials

Human Resources

Making sure that your library has the tools that will ensure the staff is properly compensated, trained, and managed

Team Building

Understanding how teams develop and work, and providing the library staff with the training to ensure they know how to work together in teams effectively

Website Development

Understanding how websites are built, keeping up with current trends in website design, acting as a focal point for website development in a library

Market Research

Understanding how to collect and analyze data to gain understanding around specific issues. A simple example of market research is using surveys at a library to collect information from patrons about a specific program idea.

Special Collections

Special collections are generally libraries with a specific focus. For example, a medical library is a special collection, as is a local history library. However, an individual library may have a special collection within it, such as genealogy or local history.

Administration

In the past, librarians would generally start working in administration after they had been frontline librarians and they didn't have special training to help them in that work. Today more and more librarians are getting training specific to administration that focuses on the business skills necessary to run a library.

Library Literacy

Teaching patrons how to use a library and its resources.

you like teaching, or do you dread the idea of having to walk students through library literacy? Do you love talking about books with library users? Your goal is to find an area that gets you excited and interested and then start learning everything you can about it. Don't do something because you have to; do it because you want to. You are trying to find an area of passion that will last for a long time.

Develop Your Own Continuing Education Plan

Your plan should define what you want to learn about your area of specialty. However, it also should identify general skills that you need to develop further. Once you have identified your areas of development, talk to your manager and get his input. He may have additional ideas because he looks at the needs of the library from a different perspective than you do.

Keep in mind that your training does not have to be formal. For example, if you are interested in readers' advisory, you might plan to spend a year going through the mystery collection at your library, learning what authors/books are in the collection. Make sure that your manager sees your goals as useful and helpful in your personal growth.

Be Proactive in Asking for Performance Feedback

Many libraries don't have a formal system set up for performance reviews. And often in the libraries that do have a process, it is ignored or done on an ad hoc basis because the process makes everyone so uncomfortable. My suggestion is to get past looking at performance reviews as chances to be criticized and look at them instead as discovering how you can do a better job going forward. Consider that if you have a performance review once a year, you'll get nerved up beforehand worrying about all the things you did "wrong" in the course of the past twelve months. Your manager will be all nerved up too, probably wanting to cover a few issues but not wanting to make you miserable in the process. Wouldn't it go much better if the two of you talked on a regular basis, so that whatever problems existed could be resolved in the moment, versus waiting (and festering) for months? Take the initiative and ask your boss for verbal feedback (a) after you've done a specific project, (b) when a specific event has happened that you want input about, (c) when you are having issues that you are trying to resolve, and (d) when you think you've done something really well. The key here is to take ownership of the need to communicate and communicate regularly. Don't wait for your manager to do this—she is probably perfectly happy ignoring the whole thing unless you make it happen in an easy and relatively comfortable way.

So how do you make a performance discussion relatively painless? If it is informal, here are a few ideas for going into the discussion prepared with the basics:

1. *Know what you want to talk about.* ("I would like to get some feedback on the program I ran on June 20.")

2. *Identify the strengths and weaknesses of your performance, giving specific support to your perspective.* ("I thought my work on the program was strong. Over one hundred and fifty people attended, surveys indicated an average rating of 4.5 on a scale of 5, preplanning incorporated all key stakeholders, and the newspapers wrote very positive reviews. The only part that didn't go well was the sound system, which was spotty and which I didn't check beforehand.")

3. *Identify key learning you got from any issues you encountered.* ("In the future I will make sure that I check the sound system twice before the author speaks.")

4. *Ask your manager what her thoughts were about your performance, or ask her for specific input about the work you were doing.* ("It seemed as though some patrons were bored. Do you think the presentation was appropriate for the audience? What might I have done differently?") Listen hard to what your manager says. Make a commitment to yourself before the discussion that you are there to listen and learn, not to rebut anything she might say. Be open to the input. You don't have to agree or disagree. Rather, try to understand what your manager is conveying and then be prepared to contemplate that input for ideas about how you might change your work (for the better) going forward.

5. *Jot down a few notes in an e-mail about your discussion with your manager and your proposed next steps, and ask your manager to reply to you if there is anything you misunderstood or didn't get right.* You are doing this primarily to ensure that you are both in agreement about what was discussed. Sometimes when things are written down, people read the comments and think, "That isn't what I meant at all!" You want to make sure that you and your manager are both in agreement as to what was said and how you are going to proceed going forward. This doesn't need to be a formal e-mail. Think of it more as just a continuation of the conversation you've already had. When you feel like you've made some progress on a particular issue, send

your manager another e-mail, letting her know. This progression of e-mails will be helpful to both you and your manager in demonstrating your ability to grow and develop in your position.

Seek Out Opportunities for Learning at Other Libraries

Librarians are generally a very collegial group. They are happy to share ideas and generally they don't mind having their ideas copied by another library (although they do like to get credit for the idea). Therefore, other librarians can become one of your best sources of training and career growth. Make a point of meeting other librarians in your geographic area and on the Web in online discussion groups. Ask questions. See if it would be possible to spend time at another library to see how they do business and to identify any ideas that might be useful at your library. Invite other librarians to come to your library for meetings. Offer to give tours of your library and as you are doing that, ask the other librarians how they do the same things at their libraries. Even if your library has no funding at all for staff training, you can always spend some time in another library and learn that way. You might even want to consider starting a formal program with several other libraries of "shadowing" or putting together librarians doing similar jobs and supporting them in the opportunity for mutual shared learning.

Look for Free Training Opportunities

There are a lot of ways to get free training. I've mentioned one already: spend time with your peers at other libraries. The following are several other ideas for getting free training, even if you have to do so on your own time:

First, search online for the term *librarianship*. There are many, many sites that provide free access to articles and seminars about the practice of librarianship. The following is a very short list to get you started. (All of these sites can be found at ipl2 at www.ipl.org.)

- *Library Philosophy and Practice* is a "peer-reviewed electronic journal that publishes articles exploring current, past, and emerging theories of librarianship and practice, as well as successful, innovative, or experimental library procedures." www.webpages.uidaho.edu/~mbolin/lpp.htm.
- *Library Stuff* is a blog "dedicated to providing resources to help librarians keep current in their professional development." The blog is sponsored by Information Today, Inc. www.librarystuff.net.

- SirsiDynix is an online resource that "provides an ongoing forum for professional development in the library field." The website sponsors weekly free Web seminars with leaders in the library industry. SirsiDynix is a corporation that develops library automation software and services. www.sirsidynixinstitute.com.

In addition to Web research, read one or more of the professional journals available in the profession. Many libraries buy at least one of these to keep staff current with trends in the industry. However, even if your library doesn't buy any of these, you can still access a great deal of the content online. Check out at least one of the following journals on a regular basis:

- *Library Journal* (Reed Business) is a trade publication for librarians, founded by Melvil Dewey in 1876. www.libraryjournal.com.
- *Booklist* (American Library Association) provides book reviews and information about happenings in the library profession. www.booklistonline.com.
- Information Today publishes several magazines focused on the library, information, and knowledge management community. www.infotoday.com.

There are numerous other library journals, most of which have at least some content provided free online. A nice compilation for further exploration can be found at www.libdex.com/journals.html.

A final resource for free continuing education can often be found at the school from which you received your library degree. Many schools offer continuing education classes but charge a fee. However, generally the fees are fairly manageable (after all, librarians are not known for having big salaries), and sometimes courses are offered for free. Keep in touch with your alma mater so that you can regularly check for these opportunities.

Find a Mentor

If you choose to spend time with your peers at other libraries, you have already started the process of mentoring, which is essentially working with others to manage your career better. However, I would recommend that you consider finding a formal mentor. Librarians are natural mentors; they work in a service profession, and I consistently find that they are usually very happy to help others in the same profession be successful. A librarian mentor can help you:

- Identify areas in which training would be helpful to your career
- Provide you with objective input about your performance as a librarian
- Help you understand the unspoken "rules" of the profession
- Provide you with recommendations for job opportunities
- Identify other individuals in the profession who might be helpful for you to meet
- Help you determine how to deal with difficult professional situations

If you want a formal mentor, you need to do some thinking before you start the process. The following are some of the items that you should consider:

What is your goal for a mentoring relationship? Are you trying to improve your performance as a librarian? Do you want to develop more contacts in the profession? Do you just need help with some specific issues? It is important to figure this out because when you identify the person who you want to mentor you, you need to be able to clearly articulate what you want from the relationship.

How long would you like this relationship to last, and how much interaction do you think you will need? It is also important to convey the amount of commitment you are asking for from your mentor. In the best of situations you will end up developing a strong, personal relationship that will last throughout your professional career. However, it is just as effective to develop a mentoring relationship around a specific purpose and once that purpose is accomplished, to reduce the amount of interaction. By telling your potential mentor your expectations, you are giving him the information to know if he can do the job effectively.

Why are you asking this individual to be your mentor? It is important to do your research before asking someone to mentor you. If you need input about how to write an article for a professional magazine, don't ask someone to be your mentor who has never done any professional writing. He won't understand why you are asking him, and he will feel uncomfortable because you are expecting help around a topic in which he is not an expert.

Once you have answered the above questions, identify who you think might meet your needs. The best-case scenario is that you already know someone who might be helpful. However, if you don't know someone, don't let that stop you. Ask your fellow librarians if they know anyone who might meet your criteria. (Now you see how helpful the criteria can be!) E-mail your library school professors and ask them for input. Keep your eye open when you visit other libraries. If you know what you want from a mentoring relationship, eventually you will run into the right person to fill that job.

Me and My Shadow

While working as assistant director at the Lucius Beebe Memorial Library in Wakefield, Massachusetts, I worked on a team with three other librarians to develop a program for library staff that facilitated a formal shadowing program with other libraries. The program was called "Me and My Shadow" and won the American Library Association H.W. Wilson Staff Development Award (given to one library nationally each year) in 2006.

The following is a summary of the program, as described in a press release. The program received great reviews from participants as being an excellent way to grow in their jobs and learn new skills. Feel free to copy the idea and find some neighboring libraries with which you can develop something similar.

The concept is simple. Match up two libraries, providing interested staff members from one library the opportunity to visit another library for a morning or afternoon. Each staff member shadows a peer in their partner library, seeing how that individual accomplishes his work and collecting ideas to take back to the home library.

The regional assistant directors' group thought the concept sounded like a good one, and four individuals (Mary Behrle, Elizabeth Dickinson, Liz Doucett, and Nancy Ryan) took on the challenge of putting together the program. The result is "Me and My Shadow," a peer-to-peer shadowing program.

The objectives of the program are as follows:

Benchmarking–give staff a chance to see how another library does its work and identify if there are any learning or improved processes that can be taken back to their own library.

Networking–give staff a chance to meet their peers in another library, develop relationships, and build contacts.

Rejuvenation–provide staff with the opportunity to re-energize their thought process about their job by being exposed to new ideas, new people, and new approaches.

To ensure that the program fosters active learning, each participant will be asked to *go with a question–come home with an idea!* All involved will be asked to identify issues or questions in their home library that they would like to find a way to address during the "Me and My Shadow" experience. At the end of their visit, each person will be asked to formally identify what she learned that might address her issues or questions. The contact person for that library will then write those ideas/learning as a blog entry that will be shared by all the libraries involved. This will allow all libraries both to communicate what they've learned and, in turn, to learn from others.

(CONT.)

Me and My Shadow (cont.)

Each library director (or assistant director) will be responsible for identifying who among their staff might be interested in shadowing a peer in another library and, ideally, acting as a host in return. All staff is invited to participate. The committee developing this program will do the following:

- Identify all libraries that are interested in participating
- Match two libraries together based on interests and provide the names of contacts at each library
- Provide a process for capturing the learning from the visits
- Provide a common blog where each library will be requested to enter their learning from the program

Each participating library director (or assistant director) will need to do the following:

- Identify a contact person for their library
- Determine who on their staff is interested in participating
- Contact their partner library and work out a schedule of shadowing
- Capture the learning from the visits via the process provided by the committee

An e-mail invitation is being sent to all regional public library directors and assistant directors. The committee will meet to match up libraries—and then the shadowing can begin!

If you take responsibility for managing your own career, the odds are good that your continuing education will go well. Don't wait for someone else to do this work. If you do, five years down the road you may find yourself wondering why you are bored.

OTHER RESOURCES

LISCareer.com. "Career Strategies for Librarians." www.liscareer.com/ education.htm.
A website with many continuing education and career development resources for librarians. The site is primarily aimed at newer librarians, and the information on it is contributed by fellow librarians.

NEWLIB-L. "The Discussion List for New Librarians." www.lahacal.org/ newlib.
This discussion list was started by the New York Library Association for librarians new to the profession who wish to share experiences and discuss ideas, issues, trends, and problems faced by librarians in the early stages of their careers. Subscription required.

THREE | NETWORKING

WHAT THIS CHAPTER IS ABOUT

Defining the concept of networking and identifying why it can be a great tool for every librarian

WHY SHOULD YOU CARE?

You became a librarian because you are interested in the profession and want to be successful at it. Networking is one of the best tools that you can use to help you be better at your job, make new connections, and build your skills so that you will be an outstanding librarian. It is another one of those tools that you should start developing as soon as you get your library degree. In fact, you should start networking while you are in graduate school, since your peers in school can be some of your best future contacts.

THE HEART OF THE MATTER

The term *networking* frequently makes people uncomfortable. You hear the word and assume it means going to a meeting with a large group of people, none of whom you know, having stilted and uncomfortable conversations with the other attendees, trying to stutter out quickly what you do for a living, and then passing out as many business cards as you can, all the while trying to think about how this person you are talking to might be helpful to you. And, in fact, that describes many of the networking meetings I've attended in my life.

Let me paint a different picture for you and see if you don't think it is more appealing. Your manager tells you that you are going to spend a morning at another library, working with the staff there. You are going to brainstorm about problems that both libraries face, you are going to see how they perform certain activities that your library wants to do more efficiently, and, along the way, you are going to have a good time meeting folks that share similar professional interests. Does that sound interesting? Guess what? That's networking.

I really dislike the term *networking.* I think it puts people off with all of its uncomfortable connotations. So let me try a new expression. In this chapter instead of networking, I'm going to talk about partnering. I define *partnering* as the process of developing relationships. It is any opportunity that lets you meet new people, gather new ideas, and help other people with their problems. Partnering is not about picking other people's brains to understand how they might help you. It is about initiating a professional relationship (which may even turn into a friendship) in which both parties are willing to provide support to each other under the theory that "we're all in this together" and "we'll all do better if we are willing to help each other." If a relationship like this works out well, it truly is a partnership between two individuals.

One of the reasons why the word *networking* makes many of us so uncomfortable is that people often don't start networking until they need or want something. In that situation, networking does become about something you want from someone else—a job, information, a recommendation. There is no relationship, no mutual support and, as a result, the whole exchange feels very uncomfortable and mercenary in nature.

However, think about when you've met someone at a professional conference that you enjoyed talking to and kept in touch with over time. You share ideas; you talk about issues you both face. If somewhere down the road that person e-mails you and asks if you know of anyone hiring reference librarians in the Chicago area, you are more than happy to help as best you can.

You won't do it because you are expecting anything in return, but because you want to help someone with whom you have a relationship. Or if a friend calls you and asks you to meet with someone they know who is job hunting, you'll probably say yes, not because you expect anything in return but because you have a relationship with your friend. I'll bet that perspective feels much more comfortable, and I think *partnering* is a better expression of the reality of the relationship.

Partnering is particularly important for new librarians. It is very easy to get so wrapped up in what happens at your new library that you forget there is a world outside that you need to keep in touch with. That wider world is important because:

- *It gives you a broader perspective.* If you work in a library where staff isn't hired that often, people can get stuck in their ways. That's bad. You want to identify many different possible ways of addressing a particular problem, not just the two methods used at your current workplace.
- *It is a good way of hearing about new opportunities.* Librarians have a great gossip network. If you are tied into that network, then it is likely you will hear about new job opportunities before they are ever posted. You can get your résumé prepared so that you are first in the door when the new job opens up.
- *It lets you make new professional and personal friends.* If you are new in a community and in a job, these relationships are important. They will be a key source of training, and they can greatly enrich your life.

How can you partner without going through the uncomfortable process noted at the beginning of this chapter? Start by volunteering at the local level of your library governance. Most libraries today are involved in some sort of consortium book sharing or book buying. Those consortiums usually have boards or committees made up of staff from member libraries to help run them. Get involved. It is a great way to meet other librarians in your state.

Consider volunteering at the state level. Find out who runs your state library association and let that person know you would like to be involved. You'll get scooped up very quickly, and you can make the situation even more productive for you by volunteering for committees focused on topics of particular interest to you.

Put together your own plan for developing partnerships. Generally, all you have to do is ask if you can spend some time observing how another library

Tips for Partnering

Keep these points in mind to help make partnering a good tool for you:

1. **Don't ever go into a situation thinking, "What can I get out of this?"** Instead think, "What needs does this person have, and can I help her?" It changes your perspective, and it means you are much more likely to develop an honest and real relationship.

2. **Keep records.** When you meet new people, find ways of keeping track of who they are and where you met them. I've learned this rule the hard way. When I started in my most recent job I probably met a hundred new people my first month on the job. I didn't keep track of them in any way, and as a result I lost the opportunity to develop those first meetings into real relationships. Find some consistent way of managing this information. "Back in the day," people used a Rolodex. Today some people use their contact list on their smart phone, develop a spreadsheet—or they continue to use paper and pencil and write it in a Rolodex. Don't worry about how to do it; just do it. What information should you track on new contacts?

   - Basic contact info if you have it: name, address, e-mail, phone
   - Where that individual works and her job title
   - Where you met the person
   - Something to help you remember that person in the future: e.g., how she looks (tall and skinny) or how she acted (very funny, told many jokes)
   - How you might follow up with her in the future: note that she was interested in *March* by Geraldine Brooks; send copy of *Booklist* book review
   - Others whom you would like to connect this individual with: note to send an e-mail to a colleague about this person. Ask if it would be OK to pass on her name and contact info, since they are both interested in starting a new book group at the library

3. **When you meet new people, find some way of following up with them after you meet them.** It can be something as simple as sending someone a quick e-mail saying, "I enjoyed meeting you," or sending him a copy of an article that you thought he might find useful, based on your conversation. (This should be something that every librarian can do!) You aren't doing this because you want anything in return; you are doing it because you had a nice conversation and you would like to maintain the relationship.

4. **Find a way to follow up in the future.** You might just check in and say, "Hi, such-and-such made me think of you. How is life going?" or you might say, "Just touching base. How are you?" Again, you are just trying to build a mutual relationship.

5. **Don't be afraid to connect people that you meet through networking.** Remember: networking is about helping other people.

works and you'll get enthusiastic support from both your library and your "partner" library. Identify what you want to learn when you go to that other library. Are you interested in developing personal skills (such as improving at doing readers' advisory), or are you trying to find new ideas and ways of working for your library (perhaps a more efficient way to process new books coming into the library)? As part of this process, it is important to identify what a successful visit to another library would look like for you, such as leaving with at least one feasible idea that you can implement in your library.

Don't limit your networking to the library world. Join local community groups too. Not only is it a good way to better understand the community in which you work, but it is also a wonderful way to develop new friendships and interests. Consider the Rotary Club or the chamber of commerce. Or if you have special areas of interest, such as athletics or mentoring kids, join a group to support them. Believe it or not, every one of those situations is a good way to build partnerships—and friendships.

OTHER RESOURCES

iLibrarian. "Hottest Facebook Groups for Librarians." http://oedb.org/blogs/ilibrarian/2007/hottest-facebook-groups-for-librarians.
A list of the most popular Facebook groups for librarians. The list can be found on the Online Education Database, which provides a guide to online and distance learning opportunities.

Levinson, Jay Conrad. *Guerrilla Networking: A Proven Battle Plan to Attract the Very People You Want to Meet.* Garden City, NY: Morgan James Publishing, 2008.
A different approach to networking, focusing around the concept of making yourself the kind of person that other people will want to meet, making the whole networking process much easier for you. I like the creative approach to the process.

LibraryThing. www.librarything.com.
A site created by readers for readers. It is a great way to keep track of the books you read, but for librarians it is also a great online social networking site where you can easily find lots of "your kind" to share information with and ask questions about your work. LibraryThing lets you catalog up to two hundred books a year, and use all its resources for free. If you want to catalog more than two hundred books, there is a fee.

Mackey, Harvey. *Dig Your Well Before You're Thirsty: The Only Networking Book You'll Ever Need.* New York: Currency/Doubleday, 1997.
Brief, straightforward information "bites" that are easy to read. The author's perspective is obviously gained from much experience. Very factual and realistic.

Teeter, Robert. "Library Networking: Journals, Blogs, Associations, Conferences." www.interleaves.org/~rteeter/libnetwork.html.
A listing by a librarian of networking resources for librarians

FOUR | MAKING "LIBRARIAN" A BRAND

WHAT THIS CHAPTER IS ABOUT

Defining branding and identifying why the job title "librarian" needs to become a new brand

WHY SHOULD YOU CARE?

In the past, the value of librarians was clearly understood in our society. However, in today's world, the role of librarian is changing rapidly, and people have a much less clear understanding of why and how librarians provide value. To counter this trend the profession needs to start telling a new story about librarians, talking about their value to their communities. In essence, we need to rebrand the concept of librarian. This chapter will explore branding and how each librarian can make an individual contribution to this effort.

THE HEART OF THE MATTER
What Is Branding?

Branding is the process of defining what makes an institution, product, service, or person unique and meaningful in the lives of its users, and sharing that message in such a way that it is noticed and has an impact. Anything can be branded. The word is everywhere today, because branding has value as a concept, being such a powerful tool for conveying information.

Why the Concept of "Librarian" Needs to Be Rebranded

The job of librarian has actually been a very strong brand for many years. If you grew up in the 1960s, a librarian was a friendly adult who would happily help you find books at your local library. A librarian was usually a woman, and she always seemed to have gray hair and be very, very smart. A librarian would talk about her job with pride but possibly not with much passion. At least in my town the librarian was strict, and you knew that if you broke the rules at the library, your mother would hear about it very quickly. As children we were afraid of the librarian in the same way that we had a healthy fear of our parents as the arbiters of our behavior.

Today there is a much less clear librarian brand. In some communities, being a librarian means that you are respected, people understand what you do, and you make a reasonable living. In other communities being a librarian means very little. People don't understand the need for a library, much less a librarian. Their perception is that you (a) hand out books, and (b) read a lot of books.

Regardless of which type of community you work in, rebranding the concept of librarian is important. If you work in a more progressive environment, you want to keep it that way. If you work in an environment of low appreciation for librarians, you want to change it. Branding can be the tool to help you accomplish both of these ends, since it will help you craft a new story about the job of librarian and then convey that story in an effective way.

How Each Librarian Can Start to Develop the Librarian Brand

Step 1: *Develop your story and be willing to be a passionate advocate for what you do to everyone you encounter.* The first part of this is easy. Librarians have a clear understanding of the work that they do and why it is important.

However, the second part is probably the toughest part of rebranding the profession. Librarians are very modest. They do their jobs quietly and well. However, keep in mind this isn't about boasting; this is about being willing to share the passion you bring to your profession with people outside your profession.

There is an easy and comfortable way of preparing your story and yourself to convey your story. Develop an elevator pitch. An elevator pitch is a very short summary of what you do (thirty seconds or less). However, it isn't a laundry list ("I catalog books, I develop story times . . ."). Rather, it is a summary of what you do *along with a summary of why it is meaningful.* The idea of an elevator pitch is to have something in your back pocket to pull out and use (not literally but figuratively) whenever someone asks you what you do for a living. You want to be able to convey that information in a short, succinct, powerful way that will grab your audience's attention so that they will remember what you've said. The following are some of ideas to help you develop your pitch:

1. Start by saying you are a librarian. This is the term that needs rebranding, but it is also a term that still has tremendous positive associations with it, particularly to older audiences. You want to tap into that power if you can.

2. If you want to, follow up the term *librarian* with very brief specifics. For example, you might start by saying, "I'm a librarian, specifically a reference librarian," or "I'm a librarian working in children's services."

3. Identify a *brief* overview of what you do. "I'm a librarian. I work in reference at the college library. The largest part of my job is selecting books for the library and helping students learn how to use electronic resources effectively." Another example: "I'm a librarian. Specifically, I work in young adult services at the public library. I help teens find books they'll want to read, and I run programs at the library designed to bring in teens."

4. Now comes the tough and most important part. *Identify something about your job that you love, that gets you out of bed in the morning, and that makes you feel like you are making a difference in your community.* This is the part of your elevator pitch that will help rebrand the role of librarian in our society—really! Using the two instances above here are examples of what I mean:

"I'm a librarian. I work in reference at the college library. The largest part of my job is selecting books for the library and helping students learn how to use electronic resources effectively. I love the fact that they walk in the door at the beginning of the semester thinking Google is the be-all and end-all of Internet resources and they walk out the door at the end of the semester understanding how to use the Internet in a smart, reasoned way—they've become real researchers."

"I'm a librarian; specifically, I work in young adult services at the public library. I help teens find books, and I run programs at the library designed to bring in teens. It's an amazing job—I have to find books so compelling and intriguing that they will hold the interest of kids raised on the constantly changing world of electronic games. I love it when I hand a teen a book, tell him a quick story about why I think he will like the book, and then ten minutes later see him comfortably slumped in a library chair, reading away."

When you have figured out what you want to say, practice saying it out loud. You might write down an idea and it looks perfect on paper, but turns out to be really hard to get through out loud. Or you might find out it is too long. Don't forget, you are trying to do this in thirty seconds or less. Ask another librarian if you can share it out loud with her. If you find that you stutter and your elevator pitch doesn't roll off your tongue, go back and look at it again. If you really believe what you are saying, it should come out smoothly and easily.

The key to a good elevator pitch is telling your story with passion, conviction, and pride and keeping it all short, short, short. You have to use your own words and your own passion. You want to make sure that your audience walks away thinking how great it is that librarians are doing such interesting work. I frequently get asked why I changed professions from business to librarianship. I tell people it's because I wanted to do something that would make a difference in people's lives. It's amazing how often I get asked follow-up questions that show a real interest on the part of the questioner.

Why is an elevator pitch important to you personally? It is always a good thing to examine your own motives for being a librarian and be able to articulate them. (You will absolutely need that skill in job interviews.) I also find it is very helpful to me when I have a tough day at work and it seems like problems are accumulating in piles around me. I stop for a second, take a deep breath, and remind myself why I'm doing this. It's a great tool for putting the world into perspective. I also like knowing how I'm going to tell the world about my job. If someone asks what you do for a living, you won't stand there with "blank brain." You already have something to say that sums up the importance of what you do.

Once you finish your elevator pitch, essentially you have developed your new librarian brand. You've articulated what about being a librarian is meaningful to your community and unique to you. You've boiled down what you want to say to a short, powerful statement and you are delivering that statement with passion and energy. That is branding in a nutshell.

Step 2: *Don't just be an advocate for librarians in ad-hoc situations. Be willing to share that information in your community in more structured ways.* If you are willing to do public speaking, then make yourself available to go out into your community and talk about what you do in your job. (See chapter 9.) Offer to talk to the local Rotary Club, at the senior center, or at the history department's biweekly meeting.

Additional Examples of Elevator Pitches

I'm a librarian; specifically, I'm the public library director in my town. I facilitate the work of the staff, manage issues that come up in the library, and work with the library board to set strategic direction for the organization. I love my job because it combines being mission-driven (helping improve the quality of life in our community) with the need to produce results that satisfies my natural inclination to be goal-oriented.

I'm a librarian. I work in the children's area of my library. I select books for the collection and run early literacy programs for young children and their parents. I love my job because I get to see new parents start to develop an understanding of why early reading is important. Then they grab onto the skills I teach with passion and energy that just lights up a room!

I'm a librarian. I work in the reference area of my library. My area of focus is genealogy. I love working with library patrons on their genealogy searches. It feels like a big mystery to me that we have to solve. It's also incredibly rewarding to see their faces light up when they finally discover who their great-grandmother was and how she came to the United States.

If you can't or don't want to do public speaking, then find other ways to advocate for your profession. Teaching a short adult education course on "Today's Library" might be a great way to share information about the library and librarian of today. If you run book groups in your library or participate in them within your community, you might suggest a book-based theme that will provide you and the group an opportunity to talk about librarians and their role in today's society. Another option is writing. Consider writing letters to the editor of your local newspaper or a student newspaper. Talk about what you do as a librarian. Identify why your work is important to you (other than your salary!). Most important, talk about why what you do matters to your community, whether it is a town, a university, or a business.

Step 3: *Identify what it is that you personally bring to your profession that is unique and important.* You've defined what librarians bring to their communities. Now you want to articulate what it is that you bring to your library. What makes you unique in what you do? Do you have any special skills that are unusual among librarians? Do you have a different type of background that might be particularly useful to users who come into your library? Do you bring a particular level of enthusiasm and passion to what you do? Spend some time thinking about this. You don't ever want to say, "I'm a reference librarian," and leave it at that. There are thousands of reference librarians in this country. What do you do as a reference librarian that is special, unique, or particularly meaningful to your community? Are you a reference librarian who loves readers' advisory and does it every chance you get? Then say that. Are you a reference librarian who also loves to teach students about the ins and outs of databases? Then say that. In this part of your elevator pitch you want to convey both what is special about your profession and what is special about you that you bring to your profession. Both are important in rebranding what it means to be a librarian.

Step 4: *Be open to constructive input from your community about what they want from their librarian.* In today's marketplace libraries can no longer simply say, "This is who we are and what we provide," and then assume people will come flocking in the door. Information sharing is no longer enough. Today, you need to be willing to have an ongoing interaction with your users and to adjust your services accordingly. (Or as an advertising executive said to me, "Marketing is not about information any more. It is about conversation.") This means that you ask people in your library how you are doing and what should you be doing differently, and then you incorporate their feedback into your work. It's a pretty simple concept, but one that we don't tend to do very often because it means we have to be open to change—and change is tough. However, the value is that if you can incorporate feedback without changing the essence of why you do your job, then you will have a strong, viable, personal brand that will have value in any library.

Step 5: *Keep yourself current and educated about what it means to be a librarian.* You don't have to learn and adopt every new concept taught in library school curriculum, and you shouldn't. There needs to be an unchanging core in your brand. However, you do need to make sure that you keep yourself relevant to the field so that your brand stays fresh. It is fairly easy to do this. Most librarians stay current by reading the library journals. Pick one or two general library blogs and stay up-to-date with them. Your MLS alma mater probably offers continuing education courses. Get the course list and see what is being taught. If you can, sign up for a course on a topic completely new

General Library Blogs

LISNews–www.lisnews.org. A collaborative weblog that covers current events in the library world. A good resource for all sorts of general information about what is happening in librarianship.

Tame the Web–www.tametheweb.com. I like this website authored by Michael Stephens, who is an assistant professor at the Graduate School of Library and Information Science at Dominican University. He is willing to think out of the box, he looks at trends and their impact on libraries, and he's interesting. What more could you want in a blog?

Annoyed Librarian–http://blog.libraryjournal.com/annoyedlibrarian/. Sometimes I get annoyed reading the Annoyed Librarian. However, I think that's a good thing, because it probably means I'm getting too set in my ways, and reading something that can be on the edgier side gets me thinking.

Bubble Room–http://blog.libraryjournal.com/bubbleroom/. Written by Alison Circle, who directs marketing communications for Columbus (Ohio) Metropolitan Library. To be honest, she gave my last book (*Creating Your Library Brand*) a good review, so I do have an innate bias on this one. However, I really do like her blog, because she is one of the few library writers I've seen who really understands marketing and business and its applicability in the library world.

to you at least once a year. If you can't do this, consider taking a continuing education course online at a source such as WebJunction. Many states provide WebJunction or its equivalent free to all librarians in the state. It's a great resource and one that you'll want to use. When possible, attend regional library conferences. Those are another great way to discover what is new and hot in the field. The idea is to make sure your brand stays relevant so that you can provide great service and ensure that you are maximizing your personal brand.

OTHER RESOURCES

Montoya, Peter, and Tim Vandeley. *The Brand Called You.* New York: McGraw-Hill Professional 2008.
> Helpful in terms of providing a step-by-step guide on how to brand yourself

Pepperdine University. "Preparing Your Elevator Speech." www.bschool .pepperdine.edu/career/content/elevatorspeech.pdf.
> Some good ideas about how to put together an effective elevator speech

Peters, Tom. "The Brand Called You." *Fast Company.* www.fastcompany.com/ magazine/10/brandyou.html.
> This is the 1997 article that really took the concept of personal branding and pulled it all together into one concept.

Schawbel, Dan. Personal Branding Blog. www.personalbrandingblog.com.
> Everything you ever wanted to know about personal branding. A little of this site goes a long way, and it provides good, free content about personal branding.

PART II HELPFUL TO KNOW WHEN YOU ARE NEW ON THE JOB

FIVE | # UNDERSTANDING YOUR NEW WORK ENVIRONMENT
Your Library

WHAT THIS CHAPTER IS ABOUT

Learning the culture of your new work environment and fitting into it

WHY SHOULD YOU CARE?

Sometimes you start a job and it is perfect. However, more often you start a job and some things are good and some things are bad. Frequently the "bad" things are due to a lack of understanding about your new library and the expectations attached to your job. If you can get a better handle on those, then frequently a so-so job will move more into the "fabulous" category—and wouldn't you prefer that?

THE HEART OF THE MATTER

Your first day on a new job (and in a new career) will most likely make you feel much the way you did on the first day of high school. You are excited,

nervous, scared to death, and thrilled to have a new job. All of these sensa-
tions are churning around inside you, so on top of everything else, you feel
sick to your stomach. Trying to figure out what your new work environment
is like and how you will become part of that culture is probably low on the
list of to-dos for the first day of work. That's OK. But on day two, you should
start thinking about it.

Staff in any organization will include leaders and followers: people who
love their jobs and will work on their day off because they enjoy it and others
who "do their time" and then go home. You may find a culture in your new
library that seeks out change and embraces creativity and innovation. You
may find an environment that values consistency and tradition and embraces
the power of knowledge gained over the long-term tenure of a career. All
of these organizational cultures can be good places in which to work. The
objective of this chapter is to help you do two things: determine the culture
of your new library, and define how you want to become part of that culture.

Let's start with some ideas about how you can start to understand the
wonderful world of your new job:

1. Listen. When you start a new job, make a commitment to keep your mouth
shut and your ears open for a period of time. Ultimately it will be important
for you to take a position on issues, to state your opinion, and to incorporate
your knowledge base into the work that you do. However, as a starting point,
listen. Listen to what your new manager says and what your new colleagues
talk about and the things that your patrons mention when they chat with
you at a service desk. Listen to what library board members say and what
your students say. Listen to what the college president says about the library.
Listen to how professors talk about the library. Think about what people are
saying and consider how you feel about their comments, but don't talk—yet.
Your goal is to get a broad sense of what your new environment is like, and
you can only do that by taking in as much information as you can. Let all that
information sit inside of you and percolate while you keep listening.

2. Stay neutral. When you start a new job and start doing all that listening,
you will find very quickly that people tell you a great deal. Partly they are
doing this out of genuine friendliness, and partly because everyone wants an
ally and supporter in the day-to-day dynamics of the workplace. Ultimately,
when you are ready to define who you are and what you want to do in your
job, you will end up being aligned with other individuals with the same perspective. That's OK and that's normal. But what you *don't* want to do is to
align yourself with any ideas or people or directions until you are ready to

do so consciously. So while you are listening and asking questions and getting a sense of your work environment, don't agree with people about issues because you like those people and want to make friends. Make friends, but don't commit yourself professionally to any ideas or directions until you are ready to do so with intent.

3. Keep lists. This one sounds stupid, but I have found it very helpful. While you are listening and staying neutral, you will be learning a lot about your workplace. Start writing down your thoughts. The process of writing your perspective down will help you begin to get a broad perspective of the culture at your new library. Write down thoughts about people you meet and meetings you attend. Write down words, descriptions, and anything that will help you get a handle on your new work world. Once a week, take time to read over what you've written. After two or three weeks you will start to

Questions to Ask Yourself

As you listen to your manager, colleagues, patrons, library board members, and students, ask yourself:

- If I had to describe the day-to-day atmosphere of this library, what words would I use? Energized, happy, low-key, dedicated, annoyed, isolated, professional, fun?
- Who are the unofficial leaders in this library? The library director is the *official* library leader. However, an unofficial leader can be anyone: a secretary, a board member, a volunteer, a children's librarian. Generally, it is someone who isn't afraid to voice an opinion. Is this informal leadership a positive or negative one?
- How does work get done? In teams or individually? Do people stick to themselves, or is there a lot of collegial sharing and interaction?
- Does this library pursue new ideas and new technologies? How are new ideas incorporated into the culture? Does staff have to advocate hard for change, or is there an atmosphere of "give it a try"?
- Is the staff young, old, young-at-heart, old-at-heart?
- Is there conflict in this organization? How is it resolved?

As you start to gather answers to these questions, you will start to understand your new work environment.

spot ideas and descriptions repeating themselves. That will be your first clue that you are starting to zero in the "real library" in which you find yourself.

It's week three and you've been listening, you've stayed neutral, and you've kept a running list of thoughts about your new job. After a certain period of time (and this time varies for every person and every job) you are going to eventually wake up some morning and say, "I get it." At that point, you'll feel like you understand your new library, your new job, and the possibilities inherent in both. Congratulations. You've done your homework right—you now get it: you understand your new work "home."

Now what? Now you figure out how you are going to become part of this world. If you like the work environment as it is and feel comfortable with it, then you want your attitudes and work process to mirror that culture. For example, if your new library is a highly energetic place with people coming and going and lots of work always to be done, you want to be an individual who is upbeat, positive, always on the move. If it is a quieter, more reflective culture, you probably want to be a bit more laid-back and calm.

A former boss of mine is an example of this perspective. At that point in my business career I worked for a highly energized, on-the-go corporation. I was new in my job and I wanted to be part of that culture. I had a great boss who was very successful and moving up the corporate ladder quickly. He told me two of his "secrets": first, he made sure that his behavior was a mirror of the corporate culture. He was perceived as a man on the move. He didn't dally around the coffee machine or sit and gossip with coworkers. He always had a place to go and work to do. Second, he identified those people who were successful, watched what they did, and then made sure his work style was reflective of theirs. If the successful people in the organization worked on team projects, obviously the ability to work collaboratively was important, so he would make sure that he was involved in team projects. He never did anything that was contrary to who he was as a person; rather, he identified the values of the organization and made sure his behavior reflected them.

If after your listening and watching you find that you've ended up in a culture that you don't like or don't feel particularly comfortable in, you have several choices about your next step:

You can choose to adjust your attitude to fit into that new culture. This isn't always bad. Sometimes we don't like an environment simply because it is new or different. With enough exposure, you can start to learn a lot of new things, and that can be invaluable in your life. In my first job after business school, I ended up working for a company that I didn't understand and in which I felt completely alien. However, I stuck it out for five years because I hate to give up (and the job did pay my bills!). That particular job ended up being one of the best learning experiences I ever encountered and one of the most productive in my life. I learned a tremendous amount about business skills and being a leader and more important, I made friends and grew in a whole new direction for me. So don't always assume that you have to change who you are to fit into a different environment. Sometimes just by being open to new thoughts and ideas, we can grow and develop in directions we might never anticipate.

You can leave that organization. Don't stay someplace that is so foreign to you that you don't see how you can ever fit in. Ideally you won't find yourself in this position, because you will have done your homework before you took

Fitting In

Here are some ideas about how you can fit into a new culture that you like and in which you want to be involved:

Socialize with your coworkers. There is nothing like spending some off-time with your fellow librarians to better understand who they are and what makes them tick. If your coworkers don't seem to socialize together, then make a point of eating lunch with them. The key is to spend time with them in a more casual environment than the library.

Volunteer to participate on a shared task in the library. This might be anything from regular contributions to a library newsletter to a special project such as setting up for a book sale. Shared experiences will help you better understand your culture and your coworkers and figure out how you want to be part of that environment.

Make a conscious effort not to talk about your last job or your time in school. As someone who has changed jobs fairly often, I've learned that one of the best things you can do to make people slightly hostile is to talk about your last library job or what you used to do. It makes people feel like you are making comparisons, and as my mother always said, "Comparisons are odious!"

Most important, don't try to do too much, too soon. The world is slow to adapt to change. As a new person in an organization, you automatically represent change whether you really do or not. Don't make your new coworkers feel like you are force-feeding new ideas down their throats. Give them some time to get to know you as a person. Once they know and respect you, they will be much more open to listening to and considering your ideas openly and thoughtfully.

the job. (See chapter 1.) But don't be afraid to admit your mistake and leave. Give yourself enough time to make sure you've really made a mistake—and then skedaddle. In today's world you don't have to stay someplace to "prove" yourself. And you don't have to work somewhere for ten years to gain credibility. The world moves much more quickly, and a short job-tenure can be explained openly and honestly. One additional note on this topic: if you find you don't like the environment of your first job, don't stay in that job and complain. Complaining about a culture does nothing for you, and it certainly won't change the culture. It is much better just to accept the fact that it isn't a good match for you and leave.

What if you wind up in a job that seems to be a mixed bag? Sometimes you understand the culture and like it, and sometimes you feel completely alien. Should you make the effort to fit in, or is the place so weird that you should get out? Here's where you need to define what is important to you in your career. Are you interested in money, learning on the job, or enjoying coworkers? What motivates you in the work environment? Once you figure out your priorities, then you can evaluate the so-so job and decide if it is helping you achieve your priorities or not.

OTHER RESOURCES

Sindell, Milo, and Thuy Sindell. *Sink or Swim: New Job, New Boss: 12 Weeks to Get It Right.* Avon, MA: Adams Media, 2006.
> A simple plan to decode corporate culture and establish your place in it during your first three months on the job. Not a book I would follow religiously, but it does provide helpful information to adapt to your own situation.

Williams, Mark. *Fit In! The Unofficial Guide to Corporate Culture.* Sterling, VA: Capital Books, 2007.
> This book provides a realistic perspective about how to understand the unspoken norms that run organizations so that you can figure out how to work inside the system.

Personal blogs.
> Do some quick research to see if any employees at your new library have personal blogs. They provide great insight into the norms of an organization, either by identifying what people love or what they hate about the place.

The library's Facebook or Twitter account.
> Both will be helpful in further discoveries about the organization's norms. (Actually, if the library has these resources, that already tells you something about it as a culture.)

SIX | **UNDERSTANDING YOUR NEW WORK ENVIRONMENT**
Your Community

WHAT THIS CHAPTER IS ABOUT

Libraries are service-oriented institutions. To understand your new work environment and figure out your role in that culture, you need to understand both the library *and* the community that it serves. This chapter is a continuation of the prior chapter and is meant to suggest steps that will help you get a handle on the essence of your service population.

WHY SHOULD YOU CARE?

By understanding the population that your library serves, you can do a better job identifying what programs and services will be useful to that population. Also, a library tends to reflect the norms of the community in which it is located. By understanding what is important to your community, you will better be able to figure out the role of your library (and your job) in that population.

THE HEART OF THE MATTER

In today's world commuting is the norm rather than the exception. There are 280 million commuters in the U.S. population. It's hard to find a job in today's marketplace where you don't have to get in your car and travel to your workplace every day.

The implication of this is that it's likely that you won't live and work in the same neighborhood or town. That can be a problem because your natural instinct is to be more involved in the community where you live than the one in which you work. When you live in a community, you become part of the fabric of that environment. If you have kids there, you learn about teachers and the schools. If you go to church there, you learn about the religious community. You read the local papers and you are aware of local politics. If you don't live in a community, you are less involved in the life of that community. For a librarian this is a problem because regardless of the type of library in which you work, you are in the business of information. Not just information about books or other resources—the questions you will get asked will cover a wide range, and more likely than not you will get asked about "things" in your community. Those things might include the names of good doctors or dentists, where to get tickets to local shows, where the nearest Dunkin' Donuts is, where the nearest food kitchen or homeless shelter is, or what politicians stand for what issues. These aren't the questions that librarians expect to get asked, but you can be assured that you will have someone ask you those questions and he will expect an answer. After all, you are a librarian, and that means you are in the business of providing information.

If you don't live in the same community in which your library is located, it is very likely that you will have absolutely no idea how to answer any of these community-oriented questions. And that means that you aren't doing what librarians are trained to do—help people by guiding them to information. This chapter is about how you can know as much as a native about your new "adopted" community to ensure that you are doing the best possible job as a librarian.

This knowledge can also have a personal impact. For my first job after library school, I lived in one community in Massachusetts and commuted to another community that is much closer to Boston. When I started that job I would have told you that it made no difference at where I lived versus where I worked. I was wrong.

My adopted community (where my library was located) was a blue-collar town that was slowly changing as housing and property taxes got more expensive. There were great upheavals in the town around rising taxes and the impact on the average blue-collar family. I didn't pay much attention, until the uproar about taxes got so loud that ultimately funding to the library was decreased and the library staff had to take an unpaid furlough to ensure that the library could manage within the new constraints. Obviously, this had a direct impact on me and my pocketbook.

If I had been more aware of the situation, is there anything specific that I could have done to change it? Probably not—the town's budget issues had been building for several years. However, by being more aware, I might have done a better job of managing my own bank account to reduce the potential impact of wage losses.

Since that time, I've learned some basic tactics to help me learn about my adopted community to ensure that I'm in touch with the community's issues. These are commonsense ideas that are very simple to follow. I do this research because I want to make sure that I have advance warning of potential issues that might affect my library or might affect me personally. I have found ten tactics for gathering the information I need to make sure I'm an informed and involved librarian.

1. When I start at a new library, the first thing I do is subscribe to the town's newspaper. I don't read the paper at the library, because I find that very quickly this becomes one of those nice-to-do but not critical tasks, and it tends to fall by the wayside whenever there are any time demands. I also don't read it online, because many online newspaper editions don't contain all of the smaller news items that make local news so interesting. I make a date with myself to read that paper every day (or as often as it comes out) and I try to do it religiously. I also try to read the paper in great detail, which for a local paper doesn't take too long. I read it in great detail because you can learn the most interesting things about a town from the small details. You'll start to learn the politics of a town, which is critical. You will begin to recognize certain names as being in the paper regularly for petty crime—and when you are a public librarian, this is also critical information. Bottom line: you'll start to understand what makes your adopted community tick.

2. I ask someone on the library staff who lives in the community (and preferably someone who is from the community) to give me a "townie" tour. If you are an academic librarian, I would translate this to getting a tour of your campus from a student. When you visit a town every day for a job, you learn the basics: where the restaurants on Main Street are, where the local grocery store is, maybe where a dry cleaner is that you can stop in at on your way home. What you don't tend to learn is the reality behind the geography. For a librarian it's very helpful to know that

Putting Your Adopted Community at Your Fingertips

It will be helpful to you to collect the following materials as part of learning about your library's community.

Get a detailed map of your adopted town or neighborhood. Make a point of regularly checking out new parts of the community served by your library. There is nothing like actually seeing a neighborhood to better understand how you can provide service to it as a librarian. Walk if you can, or drive or use public transportation if walking isn't feasible.

Get lists of your government representatives (town manager, mayor, selectmen, and state politicians). Make sure those lists have contact information for each of those individuals. Put them in the notebook. If possible attend community events where you can meet these individuals.

Get a list of where to shop and where to eat. Put those lists in your notebook and try out one of each on a regular basis.

Find a calendar of local community events and plan to attend one or two.

Find out where the local churches are and check out their websites. (Most churches now have their own web pages.) Churches are still very much centers of the community, especially in smaller towns, and understanding their role will do much to help you better understand the environment.

Collect the demographics of your community from the U.S. Census data (www.census.gov) and do a brief study of the numbers. You may find some interesting tidbits that will again add to your understanding of your community.

Do a brief compilation of the social service agencies available in your community. This will help you understand the particular issues that your community faces. For example, if you looked up social service agencies in the town where I first worked as a librarian, you would find many, many organizations dedicated to addressing mental illnesses. That is because the town had become a center for services to that community. In my town, if you look up the same thing, you'll find a large number of groups dedicated to services for seniors. This is because Brunswick has become a retirement center.

if a patron comes from a certain neighborhood, her family is probably first-generation American, or that the majority of folks in that neighborhood are very conservative financially but tend to be social liberals. Because you know that about the neighborhood, you then have a better understanding of the type of information and resources that might be particularly useful to that community. For example, in the above-mentioned case of understanding that many in the neighborhood are immigrants, it might be useful to provide information about social services or educational opportunities in the native language.

3. I try to read at least one local history book. People who live in a community and grew up there are proud of that community. Local history can help you better understand your library's users by understanding the world in which they grew up. In my first job as a librarian, I ran a book group for seniors in the community. At first I struggled to identify books that were intriguing to the participants. So I did some research on the history of that part of the community and discovered that a huge part of the local population was second-generation Italian American. As a result, they still had a huge affinity for all things Italian. Once I understood that, I was able to include books on our reading list with some relationship to Italy. They loved that tie-in, and it made them feel more comfortable with the book group as a whole. With a higher comfort level came a greater willingness to try books outside the Italian American genre.

4. If possible, volunteer to run a book group for senior citizens. Baby boomers are transient, but the generation of seniors before baby boomers tends to be much more settled. Every time I run a book group for seniors, I've found that they are a font of information about the local community. They can tell you what it was like growing up there, they will be more than happy to tell you how it has changed, and they usually love a little genteel gossiping about politics and who is doing what, where, and when. And don't hold these groups at the library—try to get into the community and meet at a senior center or retirement community. This is one of the best ways for a public librarian to get out into the community.

5. Use local stores and attend community group meetings (Rotary Club, chamber of commerce). Local stores are another great source of information about the community. When I was commuting, my tendency was to leave my job, drive to my hometown, and then do my shopping. By doing that I lost a great opportunity for hearing people talk around me, reading the local bulletin board, and finding out what's happening. Joining local community groups such as the Rotary Club or chamber is another great way of getting this feeling about your environment. You'll hear which businesses are doing well and what new projects are planned for the community, and from that type of information you can start identifying how the library might provide information and services to address.

6. Read community bulletin boards throughout your adopted town, including the one at your own library. Bulletin boards are a font of information, particularly on college campuses—but also in towns. They tell you about the cultural life of the community (posters about local music, theater events) and they tell you about social issues of interest (join Habitat for Humanity posters). Bottom line: they are a form of social barometer that can keep you clued in to the tone of your community and help you understand how your library can provide service in that environment. Many communities now have electronic bulletin boards. While they lack some of the character and interest of old-fashioned bulletin boards, they too can be a very useful way of taking the pulse of a community.

7. If you are a public librarian, take the time to identify the town's politicians. If you are an academic librarian, understand who makes the key decisions about your library. Read up on their positions. Understand whether they actively support the library or whether they view the library as a "nice to have" in the community but not a critical service. If you understand who the local politicians and decision makers are, you are in a better position to figure out how the library can better advocate for its resources.

8. If your library has local history programs, go to them. Understanding the factors that drove the development of your community will help you understand why people do and don't value your library. It may also give you more insight into how you can provide additional library services to your community. For example, in my hometown there is a small but important Lebanese community. You wouldn't be aware of that unless you understand the town's history, because most of the Lebanese are now thoroughly Americanized. However, by understanding the town's history, you could provide materials at the local library that would be much valued by that community.

9. Visit the local historical society. I recommend going to the local history society (if there is one) for the same reason that you might want to read about local history. You'll get additional insight into the community that supports your library, which in turn will improve your ability to provide relevant services and will increase your understanding of what drives the community's dynamics today. Additionally, I have found that the individuals who maintain local history societies tend to be the community's memory book. They love history and generally are more than happy to get into long conversations about what makes the community tick. You can't beat information like that when you are trying to understand the people who come to your library.

10. Plan to spend at least some of your leisure time in your adopted community. Ask your fellow librarians for ideas on how to do that. If you spend some time in your adopted community, you will start to feel much more part of the unofficial network of the community. It is amazing how much information gets conveyed between people at the grocery store, at community events, and at school events. People will come up to you and give you ideas for library programs or tell you what they like or don't like about the library. Listen carefully. Unsolicited feedback is sometimes the best way to understand what is and isn't working at your library, and you can't get that kind of input if you aren't physically available.

OTHER RESOURCES

Chamber of commerce website.
> This is an old stand by, but it is very reliable in terms of providing information about a city or town. Most chambers now have websites with helpful information in terms of providing an overview of a community. However, keep in mind that organizations have to pay to be part of a chamber, so there may be parts of the community not represented on the site.

City-Data.com. www.city-data.com.
> This site provides a detailed profile of any ZIP code in the United States. The information is based on census data, so some of the information may be redundant if you do a U.S. Census data search. However, the depth of the information is impressive and helpful.

City Guides. www.citysearch.com.

Yelp. www.yelp.com.
> On both sites, you identify the community in which you are interested and search based on areas of interest. You might enter "Portland, Maine" as your search area and "libraries" as the area of interest. There is an opportunity for

user reviews, so if you like to get information straight from the locals, these are two sites that will let you do that.

Meetup. www.meetup.com.

This site identifies different interest groups (dog owners, politics, running, skiing) to get together and share their common interests. It is a great way to meet new people in a community and to learn more about that community.

SEVEN

HOW TO MANAGE PROBLEM PATRONS IN THE LIBRARY

WHAT THIS CHAPTER IS ABOUT

Managing difficult individuals who create issues in the library

WHY SHOULD YOU CARE?

Because it is absolutely, positively guaranteed that in your career as a librarian (no matter the type of library in which you find yourself) you will eventually run into at least one individual who will create a problem in your library. Libraries are community spaces, and within any community you can find people who will create problems—and they are often drawn to public spaces to manifest those problems. If you have some tools in place to cope, this won't be a huge deal. If you are caught unprepared, it can be very unpleasant (to say the least).

THE HEART OF THE MATTER

There are always people who create problems in libraries. I don't say this from cynicism but from experience. There might be a few more in public than academic libraries because public libraries are open and accessible to all. But from my conversations with different types of librarians, I've learned that they can be found everywhere. So just make up your mind that the odds are very, very good that you will encounter "problem patrons" (as they say in the world of public libraries) at some point in your career, and for whatever reason you will be the only one in that place at that moment who can deal with the problem. You won't always be able to depend on more senior librarians or the folks in administration to take care of the problem. It will be immediate and in your face, and you'll do a whole lot better if you put a few tools in place before this happens to address the problem. This chapter is about providing those tools.

Tool 1: *Be respectful.* The first and most powerful tool is to approach all users of your library with respect, regardless of their circumstances or behavior. Assume that no one got up this morning and decided to be a problem for you personally. Also assume that everyone has worth and value. This doesn't mean that you allow bad behavior. It does mean that you treat everyone the same, recognizing that they are part of your community, and that they believe they have a perfectly good reason for the behavior they are demonstrating. Respect will go a long way toward allowing a reasonable discussion to take place between two individuals. Respect is also very important to individuals who normally don't get much of it (such as the homeless and mentally ill), and it will be particularly helpful in building rapport with them.

Tool 2: *Be informed.* When you start on your new job, make a point of asking more experienced staff members to tell you about the type of problems they encounter on a regular basis with library users and how they deal with those problems.

You'll probably have to sit through many war stories, but you'll be able to glean two things: where issues generally come from among your library's users, and what tools more experienced staff use to deal with those problem users effectively. At a college it might be students who ignore the library's "no gambling on computers" rule. Or it might be individuals who regularly sneak into the library to steal unguarded computers. In a public library it might be homeless individuals from a local shelter who use the library as their living room. Or it might be local gang members who try to use the library for drug dealing. Whatever the story is, it is good to have some sense of the cause of problems, the seriousness of those problems (gangbangers or seniors arguing over bridge games), and how the problems have been addressed in the past. You may choose not to deal with issues the same way others have, but it can't hurt to have a sense of what has been effective and what hasn't. This type of research will also help you be prepared for the first time a problem occurs.

Tool 3: *Be involved.* Make a point of watching the more experienced librarians manage difficult situations. Don't hide in the stacks when there is a problem and hope that it will go away! Your goal here is the same as with tool number two: to learn what works and doesn't work in your library. Many libraries today have a policy that if there is a problem in the facility, librarians address the problem in teams to ensure the safety of all involved. Offer to be backup for other librarians when it is appropriate, so that you can see firsthand how situations are managed in your library. An added benefit of doing this is that these encounters help you get over any initial fear you might have about this type of problem solving. Immersion therapy does work in this particular situation.

Tool 4: *Be aware.* This is a difficult tool to develop. In any library it is likely that you will have a great deal of work to do and not enough time to do it. It becomes very easy to put your head down and crank away on your work, only looking up to address library users who have questions or issues. However, being oblivious to who is in the library can be a real issue. You need to be aware of who walks into your library, what they look like, and your intuition about that individual. If you get nervous over someone walking around the library, trust your instincts. Pay attention to that individual. Be aware of what she looks like (height, hair color, clothes). If it happens naturally, say hello and make her aware that you know she is there. (People who want to cause problems frequently want to stay unnoticed.) Keep your eyes open. All of this will help you if there is a problem, and it may avert a problem before it occurs. Also, it is a great way of building your customer-service skills and making sure that your library is a welcoming, comfortable environment.

Tool 5: *Be objective.* When you observe people in your library, actively work to monitor your internal dialogue about each individual. If you find that you start automatically categorizing people by their looks (that person is obviously homeless, so he is going to be a problem), you've lost your objectivity and your corresponding ability to identify and assess potential problems. Problems can come from anywhere, not just from certain categories of people. What you need to be aware of are behaviors, not how someone looks. So if you say to yourself "that person is jittery and talking to himself and getting more and more agitated," and he is dressed like a banker, then you have maintained your objectivity. To use a librarian analogy, you are looking beyond the cover of the book to the contents—and that is what is important when you are identifying problems. Be aware of this internal dialogue and correct yourself when you find you are losing your objectivity.

Tool 6: *Be calm.* Everyone says this about difficult situations in the library and no one ever tells you how hard it is to do. Here are a couple of very basic things you can do to help maintain your calm:

Breathe deeply. A little oxygen goes a long way in counteracting the adrenaline pumping through your system in a difficult situation.

Stop and think. You can't always stop and take a moment to collect yourself. Sometimes events just move too quickly. However, if possible, stop and consider what you are going to say before you open your mouth.

Take a partner with you if you are going to deal with a difficult situation. It always helps to have backup, and after the situation is over, a partner can provide helpful input about what you did well and areas where you might improve.

When you need to give direction, do it with authority. Assume that the individual with whom you are talking will do as you ask. Approach your library users with calm authority and the likelihood is good that they will do as you ask. Don't ever be apologetic; it is your job to maintain a positive environment for all library users, not just a specific group of users. As you approach someone to discuss an issue, monitor your body language. Stand up straight, put your shoulders back, and claim the space you are in assertively—but not aggressively. Body language is a surefire way of projecting authority when done correctly.

Have a mantra with which you can encourage yourself, along the lines of "be calm, be strong." Say this to yourself if you start to feel your emotions getting the best of you. Always keep in mind that you are doing the best you can and that is all anyone can expect from you.

Practice! Put together a script that you can use for common situations and use it with fellow librarians. If you say something enough times, eventually you'll be able to be calm no matter the situation. Practice does make perfect!

Trust yourself. Believe that you can deal with any situation, and you will be able to deal with any situation.

Tool 7: *Be careful.* When you approach an individual in your library to address an issue, always think about your own safety first. There are a lot of ways to deal with problem patrons in your library (see the list of resources at the end of the chapter), but I use the old command we were taught when we were kids and learning to cross the street: stop, look, and listen.

Stop. Before you talk to the individual with the problem, stop for a second when possible, take a deep breath, and collect your thoughts. Don't be frazzled before you even begin a conversation. If one of your library patrons is mentally ill, then the last thing she needs to deal with is an upset librarian. This will only amplify and exacerbate her issues. Rather, a calm, quiet, collected approach will be much more helpful.

Look. Assess the physical situation that you are entering. You never want to end up physically cornered, and you don't want to corner the individual with the problem. Make sure you know how you can get away and that there is an avenue of escape for the other person. Again, if you feel uncomfortable, trust your intuition. Keep a distance between you and the person you are addressing so you both feel more comfortable. When possible, take another staff member with you. I always ask my backup to stay in the background and remain unobtrusive so that the person with whom I am talking doesn't feel overwhelmed by attention.

Listen. Start by listening to the person with the problem. Don't formulate answers before the person is done talking. Really listen to what they are saying. Frequently, the fact that someone is truly listening and giving them time diffuses the anger of a lot of individuals, particularly the homeless and mentally ill. However, at the same time that you are listening to that person, listen to your own intuition and pay attention. Do you feel unsafe or uncomfortable in this person's presence? If so, there is probably a good reason even if you can't put your finger on it. Don't put yourself in a place (like an office) where you will be alone. If you feel like someone is about to explode and lose it, pay attention to that feeling. Get the police involved. I always tell the staff at my library that if calling the police even crosses their minds for a particular issue, then call the police. Their intuition is telling them something important.

Tool 8: *Be able to laugh.* Don't take the world, your job, or yourself too seriously. Whenever it is appropriate, I try to bring humor into difficult situations because I find it can do a tremendous amount to diffuse tension. I also find it is a wonderful way of getting past a problem that has occurred and been addressed. It is also tremendously helpful to be able to laugh at yourself when you are dealing with teens and young adults. However, be careful about using humor inappropriately. When someone is really upset or is having a mental health issue, he wants to be taken seriously, and if you attempt to diffuse the situation with humor, he may feel slighted. Gauge the situation carefully before bringing out the jokes!

Tool 9: *Be thorough.* When you are addressing a problem patron, be willing to invest the time necessary to identify the real issue. If the issue is not something you can personally address in the moment, you will have to tell the patron that you will talk to your manager about the problem and that either you or the manager will get back to the patron. If this is the situation, you will need to make sure you have all the correct facts in hand before discussing the issue with your manager. This is will ensure that an appropriate decision can be made.

Tool 10: *Be finished.* Sometimes you will have an issue with a regular library user. It may be someone having a bad day, or a student who is unhappy with a policy. In any case, it is someone you know and with whom you have regular interactions. Once you've dealt with whatever the issue is, be prepared to let it all go. Don't hold grudges and don't assume behavior on one day will predicate specific behavior on another day. Accept that the past is past and assume that in the future all interactions with that particular individual will be fine.

OTHER RESOURCES

Professional courses or sessions.
Managing difficult individuals in the library is an ongoing topic of discussion among librarians. Most local and state library groups will offer at least one or two courses on this topic at annual meetings. ALA offered a course at their 2009 Annual Conference in Chicago, and it was standing room only.

Davis, Warren Jr. *Black Belt Librarians: Every Librarian's Real World Guide to a Safer Workplace.* **Charlotte, NC: Pure Heart Press, 2006.**
A simple, commonsense approach to safety in the library for librarians

WebJunction. Handout from "Dealing with Angry Patrons" LibraryU Course. www.webjunction.org/c/document_library/get_file?folderId=20191474 &name=DLFE-4610002.doc.
As part of the course on managing problem individuals in the library, WebJunction puts together a nice list of resources on the topic.

Your local police force.

Consider inviting a representative from your local police force to a staff meeting to talk about how they manage difficult individuals. Police are trained in managing problem individuals, and they use good techniques that can be equally valuable to librarians.

EIGHT | MANAGING CONFRONTATION PRODUCTIVELY

WHAT THIS CHAPTER IS ABOUT

Identifying tools that will help you be comfortable confronting others when necessary and dealing professionally with situations in which you are confronted

WHY SHOULD YOU CARE?

The saying is that death and taxes are the only two things in life of which you can be sure. I would add the need to confront another individual in your career as another element of life that you know will happen at some point. This chapter will provide you with tools to allow you to manage confrontations professionally and positively.

THE HEART OF THE MATTER

Almost no one *likes* confrontation. It is a scary situation, trying to be honest with another person about something they are doing or saying that you don't like. Your heart races, your mouth dries up, and your eyes might tear up. No one enjoys those scenarios.

On the positive side, confrontation allows all parties involved to put their thoughts out in the open where everyone can see them. I'm a firm believer that by putting issues out in the open, they become much less scary and much more manageable. However, I also think that confrontation can only be productive if both parties in the discussion are professional and open to listening. Otherwise, confrontation is only about one person venting and letting off steam with no productive end result in sight.

Sadly, productive confrontation isn't a skill that is taught at any of the schools I've attended. Productively managing confrontation is something I've had to learn on my own through trial and error (a lot of error!). The following is my twelve-step process for getting through a confrontation productively and professionally.

Step 1: *When issues arise between you and another person, address them immediately before they result in the need for a major confrontation.* In other words, don't let things slide, allowing molehills to turn into mountains. It is a lot easier to have a quick chat with someone about a small problem than to ignore the problem until it turns into something big and scary. Our natural desire is to ignore issues in the hopes that they will go away. As someone who has done this many, many times I can assure you that the issues never go away; they just get bigger.

How do you start a discussion like this? My recommendation is to be straightforward but also respectful of the other person's feelings. So I might say to someone, "It seems like our interactions aren't going very smoothly. Can we sit down, talk about what isn't working, and figure out how to go forward more effectively?" In this opening I'm not accusing anyone of bad behavior or of being a jerk or creating problems. In fact, I'm not identifying any issues other than the fact that I would like to make our work together be more effective. I'm consciously trying to keep things at a fairly objective level, and I'm focusing on the desired end result (a smooth work process) versus on the person.

Be aware that this opener might not work if you are dealing with someone who is highly conflict-averse. At one point in my career, I asked one of my coworkers if we could sit and talk about our obviously very rocky relationship with the goal of trying to make our two departments work more effectively together. It had taken me a long time to get up the nerve to have this conversation, and I had spent a lot of energy getting ready for what I knew would be a difficult discussion. Imagine how deflated I felt when he told me that he didn't know what I was talking about and as far as he was concerned we had no problems or issues. It was patently not true, but I had no idea how to proceed, so I stuttered and hemmed and hawed and then left the room. This was a perfect deflection on his part. He took all the wind out of my sails and made it clear that we had nothing to discuss.

Unfortunately, I let things continue that way for some time until our relationship was so uncomfortable that our issues couldn't be resolved. Since then, as I've worked in other jobs and gained a certain degree of maturity, I've formulated what would have been a better approach.

- I would acknowledge his feelings as legitimate: "Great. I'm glad to hear that you think things are going well."
- However, I would not drop the discussion. Instead, I would identify one or two situations in which obvious problems arose because of our relationship and the implications of those problems on your work environment. Then I would ask him if he agreed those were problem areas, with the goal of getting him to acknowledge that everything wasn't as smooth as he indicated.
- Finally I would ask if we could talk about the specific situation, with the goal of figuring out how to avoid anything like it in the future.

While you might need several such discussions to resolve issues with the "passive avoider" personality, at least in this situation you are keeping the interaction going and, I hope, eventually getting to the heart of the problem.

Step 2: *If an issue does turn into something big and out-of-control, acknowledge to yourself that you can't avoid a confrontation and it is the only way things will get resolved.* I'm an expert at ignoring problems and hoping they will go away. But now when I identify a potential issue that will need to be confronted, I set a timetable for myself to determine when I will address the issue. This keeps me from avoiding something until it gets to be the size of a house. For example, I will determine that in one week, if the problem hasn't started being resolved, I will have to have a discussion with so-and-so to resolve the problem. On the date in question I sit down and think carefully about whether I've seen any progress on the problem. If not, I move on to the next step.

Step 3: *Before you talk to the individual with whom you are having a problem, spend some time thinking about what the issues really are.* Take that particular person out of the situation and try to identify the behaviors you don't like, rather than the individual that you don't like. Determine how the behavior is affecting both of you in the workplace. If the problem is simply that you don't like someone, then the solution is simple: you need to deal with your emotions to ensure they don't affect your work! However, if the problem is that person A does not communicate the status of a project when there are issues that need to be resolved, then this is obviously something that will affect your workplace and will need to be addressed. Try to separate the personal from the professional and focus on the professional. It is harder to argue with someone who says, "We need to do this because it will make the library run better," than with someone who says, "I don't like you. You are a jerk!" Whenever possible try to take the emotion out of a conflict and insert the intellect.

Step 4: *Practice.* Write out what you want to say. You aren't going to memorize anything, but I do find that writing issues out tends to help you clarify them. Then say what you want to say out loud. Again, you may say it totally differently when you get in front of the person you need to confront, but this process will give you a great deal of self-confidence in your ability to speak precisely and effectively. If it would help, get a friend to listen to you and tell you where you are veering from the professional into the personal.

Step 5: *Keep your manager in the loop and ask for advice and input.* It is always useful to get a check on what you are doing and saying in a conflict situation. (I've avoided seriously sticking my foot in my mouth several times by doing this.) By keeping your manager informed you will ensure that you have her support and help. It also indicates to her that you are confident in your abilities to deal with this problem, but you are also still cognizant of the need for support around the issue. If the other person in your discussion decides to react unprofessionally by talking to your manager, then you have covered your bases and your manager knows you are doing your best to resolve a problem and not make it worse.

If your manager is the person you need to confront, you might want to talk to the human resources person in your library. If you don't have one, ask a librarian who you can trust to be discreet to give you feedback.

Step 6: *Meet with the individual in question in a neutral space where you won't be interrupted and where there won't be an audience.* You don't want to be in the position of "begging" a coworker to help you deal with a problem. And you don't want to demand that a coworker help you with a problem. Rather, you are trying to get together as peers to find a solution that will make your workplace run more effectively. Therefore, find a place to meet where you are equals and where the power dynamics inherent in location has no ability to make either one of you feel uncomfortable. Also, you don't want to have this discussion in front of other people. An audience always changes the dynamics between two people, sometimes for the better but more often for the worse. One person is very likely to start "playing to the audience" and thereby avoiding the real issues.

Step 7: *Start the conversation by acknowledging that there are always two parties in a problem.* Identify what you think is driving your behavior. Don't talk about people or their personalities, even when you might be dying to tell the other person exactly what you think of him. Rather, talk about what you think is causing your problems and how it affects your work: "When you don't pass on important e-mails to me, it makes me feel unimportant and unacknowledged for my expertise. As a result I tend to avoid communications from you, and then work doesn't get done."

Be willing to own your own behavior. However, don't make the mistake of owning all of the bad behavior that has happened, which the other person in your discussion might want you to do. It always takes two people to start a conflict.

Manage Your Emotions

You can probably write a whole book on managing the emotions inherent in a confrontation. I think the best tool for managing the anxiety and stress of a confrontation is preparation. If you are confronting someone else, do the work to get your thoughts clarified and in order before you get into a discussion with them. You'll find that the more you involve your intellect, the less room there is for your emotions to take over. I also find that the more you truly try to listen to the other person with no agenda other than understanding his perspective, the better chance your intellect will have to control your emotions. However, understand that all of your emotions are honest and you shouldn't worry too much about them. Just don't let them take control and eliminate your ability to be professional and appropriate.

Step 8: Listen. This is the tough part. When you have stated your case, close your mouth and listen. Don't formulate what you are going to say next as the person is talking. Just listen and see if you can understand what he is saying and why he is saying it. Don't respond to accusations of bad behavior or of something you did six months ago that created the problem. Just listen.

Step 9: Listen. It's tough to stress this one too much. Listen to the other person openly and with no effort to formulate a response. Your goal is to truly put yourself in the other person's shoes and see if you can understand where the problem comes from in his eyes. The sooner you can understand the other person's perspective, the more likely you will be to find an answer to the conflict. This is probably the toughest part of any conflict, because you are probably going to hear (at least at the beginning of this discussion) all of the reasons why you are an awful person and all the things you've done wrong. Here's where you really need to hold on to your emotions and try hard not to get defensive.

Step 10: *Try to move past "I did this, you did that" to agreement on the problems.* A statement that can be helpful in this respect is to say, "What you are discussing happened in the past. We both acknowledged that it happened. Now how do we move forward to find ways of making sure it doesn't happen again?" Don't be drawn into a "yes, you did; no, I didn't" discussion. There is no way to win that kind of interaction, and it will only lead to bad feelings and bad energy. Instead, focus on getting to agreement as to problem identification. This is a productive use of time and energy, and most people are usually willing to move in that direction. Make sure that you both agree on the real issue that you are trying to address. This is core to getting to a productive solution.

Keep Things Confidential

Don't discuss your confrontation with anyone except your manager. If you do, you risk losing any trust that you built with the other person in your confrontation. It is important that you both feel there is shared honesty, openness, and a willingness to keep the discussion between the two of you. If you need to discuss the confrontation with your manager (or anyone else), tell the other person that you must do that. Ask if she is OK with the sharing or if she foresees any problems in doing so. Respect her perspective as much as you can without jeopardizing your relationship with your manager.

Follow Up with Notes

Immediately after having the discussion, write out your interpretation of the events. Ask the other individual to review what you've written and to identify any areas of disagreement. This ensures that you both have the same starting place for moving forward. It also gives each of you a document that you can share with your manager(s) as to how you will move forward.

Step 11: *Problem-solve.* Once you've reached agreement on the problem you are facing (we don't communicate well and that creates tensions in our department), spend some time brainstorming ideas about how this problem might be resolved (daily check-in sessions, weekly reports to each other, weekly lunches with each other). As a team, think about the pros and cons of each solution and then together agree which solutions you will both implement. Also, set up a time when you will meet again and review how the problem resolution is working. This last step is important because it will give you the forum for resolving any subsequent problems that might crop up as you implement solutions.

Step 12: *Go to your manager with your results.* Get advice and feedback. It is important that you and the individual with whom you are having a problem follow up your discussion with your respective managers. You want to make sure that your manager is comfortable with your problem-solving, and you also want to make sure you've identified all of the key issues.

Conflict is tough no matter how good the process you put in place to address it. Understand that you will make mistakes and that not all conflicts can be resolved. Sometimes the disparity between the two points of view is too great to resolve. At that point, you either have to be able to live with—and act professionally with—the ambiguity of an unresolved conflict, get a more experienced person to help you resolve the conflict, or move to a different work situation where the conflict will no longer be an issue. While sometimes the third option is the only choice, I would strongly encourage you not to take that direction until you have made an honest and concerted effort to address the problem. If you have done that, then I think you can leave knowing that you tried your best. If you haven't done that, then you won't have developed your conflict resolution skills any further, and it is likely you will just encounter another situation in the future that has to be resolved.

OTHER RESOURCES ————————————————————————

Pachter, Barbara, and Susan Magee. *The Power of Positive Confrontation: The Skills You Need to Know to Handle Conflicts at Work, at Home and in Life.* New York: Marlowe and Company, 1999.
A practical, detailed guide, illustrated with many real-life situations that clarify the author's perspective

Ursiny, Tim. *The Coward's Guide to Conflict: Empowering Solutions for Those Who Would Rather Run Than Fight.* Naperville, IL: Sourcebooks, 2003.
The title resonated with me, and I liked the fact that this book talks about a difficult subject with humor. I also like the checklists provided by the author as a way to work through his process.

NINE | **PUBLIC SPEAKING**

WHAT THIS CHAPTER IS ABOUT

Defining why it is important for a librarian to know how to speak publicly and identifying some of the tools that might help you be an effective public speaker

WHY SHOULD YOU CARE?

You can't avoid it forever. At some point in your life as a librarian you will have to speak in public. Learning how to do it effectively (if not happily) will eliminate a lot of fear and anxiety and will be a big help to you in your career.

THE HEART OF THE MATTER

You've heard the statistic: more people in the United States fear public speaking than they fear death. The fear of public speaking haunts many of us; it can be truly debilitating, bringing on stuttering, blushing, shaking hands, a nervous stomach. I'm a perfect example of this—I'm someone who considered getting kidney stones a much better option than public speaking.

If I understand at a personal level how awful public speaking is, why on earth would I recommend that librarians learn this skill? I have a very simple reason: mastering this skill will definitely make you a better professional and will probably make you a better person. Let me explain.

I'll start with the better professional part. Any librarian who thinks that she will never have to perform public speaking is just plain wrong. In some way, some place, some capacity, you will be asked to talk in front of a group. I can guarantee it, no matter whether you are a public or academic or special librarian. You may be asked to take a group of schoolchildren on a tour through your library, or you might have to convince your fellow librarians about the need for specific equipment at your library. You might have to teach college kids how to use electronic databases, or you might have to stand up in front of your library's board of directors and tell them why spending money on a program makes sense. You can either spend a lot of time and energy avoiding public speaking, and then dread it when inevitably you find you have to do it, or you can find a way to speak effectively and competently so that you demonstrate your skill as a professional. And librarians are, above all, professionals, so I'm guessing this reason might have some draw.

There is another good reason to learn public speaking that is very personal. I am a master at avoiding my fears. But gradually I have learned that when you face down a fear and manage it, it is one of the most empowering things you can do for yourself. No matter what stage you are in life or in your career, it is a wonderful thing for your self-confidence and personal satisfaction to know that you have faced down a terrible monster—and found it really wasn't all that terrible. Learning how to do public presentations can do this for you—really.

How do you know if you need to work on your public speaking skills? This is an easy one to figure out. First, do you ever speak in public in any capacity? If the answer is no, then you need to get to work. If you do speak in public upon occasion, then ask yourself the following: "Do I get any physical 'symptoms' before speaking in public, like an upset stomach, sweaty palms, shaky hands (my own personal favorite), rapid breathing, or a choking feeling in my throat?" If your answer is yes, then this chapter is for you. If you answered no, then good for you. You've figured out how to speak publicly in a way that your body can tolerate without making you crazy.

If I'm such a chicken about public presenting, where do I get the chutzpah to tell you to do it? I can because I'm proof that you can make this change in your life. In the past ten years I've learned how to talk comfortably in front of groups of three or thirty or three hundred people, and I even enjoy myself. But this change didn't just happen like a bolt of lightning out of a clear blue sky. I spent a lot of time and energy working at it, trying different options until I found one that worked for me. I hope that by sharing some of what I learned, you can accomplish this same change much more quickly and effectively. Fear of public speaking is a very personal fear and therefore will generally need a personal solution; this isn't going to be one of those one-size-fits-all answers. But my experience should give you some effective tools to help you draw your own map.

I found two tools that worked for me. My first tool was—believe it or not—Dale Carnegie classes. Yup, good old Dale Carnegie that has been around since the 1930s. Dale Carnegie of *How to Win Friends and Influence People* fame. I don't want to be an advertisement for this system, but for me it was incredibly effective. (You can research today's Dale Carnegie by going to www .dalecarnegie.com.) Here's what I think made the classes so helpful for me:

When I went, you had to go to classes once a week for thirteen weeks, and you couldn't skip a class. The repetition, or what you might call "aversion therapy," was a big part of what helped. You had to do some sort of public presentation in every single class. I was scared to death for the first class and second class and third class. By the fourth, fifth, and sixth classes, I was starting to calm down. Through sheer repetition my body started getting tired of having all those physical reactions to public speaking. And amazingly, when your body isn't blushing and sweating and your pulse isn't racing and your mouth isn't dry, the public speaking part actually gets pretty easy.

So the lesson here is, find a way to do public speaking every single week. It doesn't matter if you force yourself to say a few sentences at a staff meeting, or go to public meetings and speak up for a cause you can believe in, or sign up for a course like Dale Carnegie. Make a point of speaking in front of people, over and over and over. Yes, you will be terrified the first, third, and even fifth or sixth time. But at some point, your body will get bored with having to come up with all those physical reactions, and it will start to get easier. Really.

At the Dale Carnegie classes I attended, we were asked to talk about personal issues in front of the class. In many ways this is easier than business speaking, because you are talking about what you know best: you. No one else knows more about you. You are the expert on you. When you finally understand that you are the expert in the room, you stop being afraid. The lesson I took away from this is to always make sure that you are prepared when you do a presentation. Go over your material time and time again.

(Don't memorize it, but make sure you have total comfort with what you are presenting.) You will find two things when you finally present: that your nerves are less because you are so comfortable with the material, and that truly understanding that you know something your audience doesn't puts you in the position of helping them—and there is nothing to take your mind off your own problems like helping someone else.

Finally, you were required to talk at least once in each Dale Carnegie class on the spur of the moment with absolutely no preparation. This was probably the hardest thing any of us did. What I learned from that was to stop, take a deep breath, and ask our teacher to clarify the topic if I needed a moment to collect myself. This lesson is a critical one: understand that you don't ever have to start talking publicly until you are comfortable and ready to do so. You are never out of control unless you allow yourself to be. It's amazing how comforting it is to know that when someone asks you a question, you don't have to just blurt out the answer. You can take a breath, take a drink of water, ask questions, even walk around!

The second tool that worked for me was that I stopped approaching public speaking as a formal "presentation" and started approaching it as a teaching opportunity. I looked at every presentation that I did as a chance to teach my audience something important. Because I am a librarian and one of the things librarians do very well is to teach (and help) others, this helped me change my perspective enough that I could manage my fears. I would start by asking myself as I was putting together a presentation to identify the two or three things that I wanted to make sure my audience learned. Then I would craft my presentation to make sure that I was getting my ideas across. This included making sure that my audience was involved and participating in the learning process. By focusing my energy out toward the audience (versus inward in a constant process of monitoring and measuring my own nerves), I started to get past my fears.

The following ten tips are some of what I learned as I started to get more comfortable in public speaking:

1. Find other folks in the same boat and join them. That means attend classes like Dale Carnegie or join a group like Toastmasters. Everyone is in the same boat (they all hate speaking in public), so you will never find a more empathetic audience. They will cheer you on when you stumble, help you out with ideas, and be a great resource long after the class is over. You will be amazed what you will do in a supportive group that you would never, ever try on your own!

2. Be your own best audience. Develop your presentation and then present to yourself out loud at least ten times. That's right, ten times. You will find that every time you go through a presentation out loud that you will find ways of saying something more effectively. By the tenth time, you will be very comfortable with your content and your delivery. That will greatly help alleviate your nerves. As you get more comfortable with presenting, you will find the degree to which you need to practice out loud. I've discovered that I practice out loud until I'm bored. Once I'm past nervous and getting bored, then I know that I'm ready.

3. Don't EVER read a presentation to an audience, no matter how scared you are. The odds are good that everyone in your audience (unless they are toddlers or you are teaching a literacy class) can read on their own. Being read to in a presentation is annoying and will turn off your audience. To help make sure that you don't fall into reading when you are nervous and starting a presentation, make sure your first few slides are just pictures—no words. This can be a little scary, but if you have practiced as we discussed, you'll know what to say. Actually, that's a good one for tip number four.

Quick Practice Ideas to Get Over Your Fear

Everyone has to go to staff meetings. Try to make at least one contributory comment at every meeting you attend. Don't just talk out loud for the sake of talking. Keep track of the discussion and work to find a way to add to the content.

Ask your children's librarian if you can do a very short presentation to the little kids at a story hour about something you love. You might read them your favorite story, play an instrument for them, or even bring in your dog and show them a trick that the dog can do. It almost doesn't matter; if you are excited, little kids get excited. And there is nothing better to give you a sense of perspective about public speaking than to do it with young children.

Most churches today have laypeople read a scripture during the service. If you go to church, offer to do the reading on a Sunday. It's getting you in front of an audience, but it would be tough to find a friendlier, more supportive audience!

4. Use pictures, not words, in your presentation visuals. PowerPoint is a wonderful tool. It helps keep an audience focused. But it has led an entire generation of Americans to write out presentations in great detail and then read them to their audience—and then call that a presentation. I can think of nothing more boring or less likely to teach your audience anything. Instead, think about how you could translate each key point in your presentation into a picture. Put that picture on the slide and then use the picture to reference your key points. People will remember the picture and by remembering the picture, they will remember the content. A picture really is worth a thousand words.

5. Don't be afraid to be afraid. Public speaking is uncomfortable, and I think the folks who tell you to ignore or get rid of your feelings are nuts. It just isn't that easy. A much better approach (in my mind anyway) is to tell people to accept that they will be nervous and to accept that it's OK to be nervous. Somehow the very act of accepting that you are nervous, instead of trying to get rid of those nerves, helps you start putting your fear in perspective. Yes, you are nervous. Big deal. No one really cares or notices but you, and if they do notice, the odds are good that they will be supportive because they've probably been there too. Get over it and get the job done.

6. Make a commitment to pursuing the goal of improving your public speaking skills and don't give up. You can do it, but it requires an honest effort. Put together a strategy about how you are going to do this. Don't worry if the strategy will take several years to accomplish. Just get started.

7. Be willing to experiment. What worked for me might not work for you. Be open to new ideas and new ways of approaching this opportunity.

8. Ask friends and colleagues what they have tried and how it worked for them. The step that finally worked for me came from my brother-in-law: if you go to a presentation and hear a good speaker, take the time after the presentation to ask her how she learned to be such a good speaker. People have many different ways of coping with fear of public speaking, and you'll probably get some great tips.

9. Find opportunities for public speaking, no matter how small. This is the hardest one for those of us on the shy side. If you don't normally talk in a staff meeting, start raising your hand. If you avoid asking questions in big groups, give it a shot. Find low-risk opportunities for talking publicly as often as you can. The repetition will eventually dull your body's physical reactions to the process.

10. Make a commitment to keep track of every occasion that you do public speaking, large or small, over a six-month period. Keep a notebook and track when you speak publicly, regardless of the context. Write down something positive about the experience. ("I didn't throw up beforehand.") Write down the absolute worst thing that happened. ("I forgot my name in the middle of the presentation.") Write down anything that happened as a result of the worst thing. ("A couple of folks kidded me after the presentation about my blanking on my own name.") At the end of six months, go back and read the notebook. I can guarantee two things: you'll notice that most of the "bad" things weren't really that bad, and that even when you do something "bad," there very rarely are any repercussions! This helps you start to get a sense of perspective about public speaking (no, the world won't end if your hands shake a little), and perspective is the beginning you need to manage those nerves.

For me the process of getting rid of my fears didn't happen overnight. It took me a good two years once I finally found the right combination of attitudes and tools that worked for me. That is the third piece of advice that I can provide: don't give up. If you are really committed to changing this part of your life, you have to be prepared to work at it and work at it. But if you do, I can guarantee that while the nerves will probably never go away totally, you will start to be much less concerned about those nerves and much more concerned with enjoying your presentation process.

OTHER RESOURCES

Desberg, Peter. *Speaking Scared, Sounding Good: Public Speaking for the Private Person.* Garden City Park, NY: Square One Publishers, 2007.
This book talks a lot about the psychological aspects of public speaking. I think it is helpful because if you know why you are afraid, often it reduces the fear.

Dlugan, Andrew. "Six Minutes: Public Speaking and Presentations Skills Blog." http://sixminutes.dlugan.com.
A great blog on this topic. Every week this blog identifies the best public speaking articles that the author finds on the Web. In addition, he provides reviews for books on public speaking that I found particularly helpful.

Finally, he identifies other blogs that focus on public speaking—an invaluable tool for getting additional information on the topic compiled nicely in one location.

Lucas, Stephen E. *The Art of Public Speaking*. New York: Random House, 1989.
This book is focused less on getting past your fears and more on the nuts and bolts of how to write an effective presentation, including finding a topic, organizing your materials, and various tools to use in the body of the speech to keep it interesting. It is considered a classic on the topic, but if you are comfortable with the process of collecting and organizing your subject matter, this book is probably less useful.

Toastmasters International. www.toastmasters.org.
Toastmasters can be found throughout the United States, or you can go online to find a group meeting. Toastmasters are groups that get together every week to do public presentations for each other and find ways of overcoming members' public speaking fears. I like Dale Carnegie and Toastmasters, because in both groups, the folks who teach you have (or had) the exact same fear as you, but have found a way to overcome it. Both groups also provide a structured environment that gently forces you to confront your fears—and isn't that what you really want?

TEN | TEAMWORK

WHAT THIS CHAPTER IS ABOUT

Defining teamwork, exploring what it looks like at a library, and identifying basic tools that will help you work effectively on teams at your library

WHY SHOULD YOU CARE?

Much of the work done at libraries is done in teams and through the use of consensus decision making. Understanding how to negotiate this process smoothly will greatly improve your ability to work effectively.

THE HEART OF THE MATTER

Working in teams can be fun. It can also be complete agony, especially if the team is composed of individuals who don't know how to work in teams. There are many, many resources available to help build your skills as a member of a team. What I've identified here is some basic advice that might be helpful.

Here are my thirteen tips for being a good team player:

1. Spend some time getting to know your team members. If you are going to spend a lot of time with your team, knowing who they are and how they think will be very helpful to the process of getting work done. Suggest that your team have a brown-bag lunch before the real work gets started. Or catch dinner together after work. It doesn't really matter what you do; the key is to spend enough time together so that everyone stops being just team members and starts being real people.

2. You will need to take on a role on your team and you might not be the team leader. That's OK. On teams of inexperienced team players, I've found that almost everyone on the team feels they should take on the role of leader, and that being team leader is the only role of any real importance. That just isn't true. Team leaders are important. However, they aren't any more or less important than anyone else on the team, despite what you may see or hear on television. In addition to team leaders, all teams need someone who can help facilitate discussions, someone who is good at keeping track of information, someone who likes to do research, and someone who doesn't mind the job of pulling together the final work product. Each of these roles are just as important as team leader, so if one of them seems to fit your personality, focus on that job and don't worry about not being the team leader.

Team Leader Responsibilities

- Identify when and where a team will meet
- Clarify who is taking on which role on a team: "Mary, it sounds like you enjoy doing research. Would you mind picking up that role on this team?"
- Help the team clearly define its goals and figure out how it will measure success
- Keep the team moving forward. If the team runs into conflict, help facilitate a discussion about what caused the conflict and then move the team toward resolution.

3. Teams go through periods of growth and adaptation, just like any relationship. That's OK too. I have never been on a team that didn't go through the traditional "storming" phase. Storming is when conflict arises within a team, and the conflict can be about almost anything. It might be about the approach to the issue at hand; it might be about how much work a particular team member is or is not doing; it might be about the color of the paper used in a presentation. Storming is a normal process that a team needs to go through to be able to work together effectively. Boundaries need to be established, roles need to be defined, and each person on a team has to understand how the other members of the team work. If your work team, which seemed to be moving along effortlessly, suddenly has a huge argument, don't panic. Just get back together, address the issue, and start working together again. It's all normal.

4. Listen. Listening is a critical responsibility for all team members, and it is the one most frequently ignored. Teams will not move forward if every person on the team has his own agenda and isn't willing to adjust that agenda to meet the needs of the team as a whole. Additionally, listening is a wonderful way for each team member to increase his own learning. You can always learn from others on a team (even if what you are learning is what you don't want to do in the future). Here are a couple of ways to tell if you are listening:

- As someone else is talking, monitor your reactions. Are you spending most of the time he is talking formulating your own response? If so, you aren't listening.
- Are you having an argument with the speaker even as he speaks? Again, you aren't listening.
- Are you thinking to yourself, "What an idiot!"? Guess what, you aren't listening.

Make a commitment to practice your listening skills by focusing 100 percent of your attention on your team members as they speak. Don't formulate a response, don't critique what they are saying—just listen. Then take two seconds to reiterate to the speaker what you heard him say. "So, if I heard you correctly, you said that . . ." This is a very helpful tool to make sure that not only did you hear your team member, but that you understood what he was saying.

5. When you are working on a team, be prepared to put in 110 percent effort. Don't ever try to coast on the work of team members. They won't forget. I have never encountered a team that didn't have certain expectations of all its members. Make sure that you understand those expectations and can meet them. If for some reason you will not be able to perform at the level the team expects, talk to the team as a whole about why not. If the team is in agreement about your not meeting expectations, then the situation will still be workable. However, you never want to skimp on the work. Everyone will know what you are doing, and you will make a lot of people angry and even more importantly, they won't forget.

6. Be willing to push the team. The opposite side to the above point about giving 110 percent is that as a team member you absolutely have the right to tell the team or individual team members when you think they are not contributing the appropriate amount of work. You also have the right as a fully functioning team member to push the team to work harder, do more research, or spend additional time on a project. A team's end result is generally as good as the expectations of the most exacting team member, so if you feel things are not as good as you want them, push the team to higher levels of production.

7. Don't hide your ideas or thoughts. If you have a great idea, bring it out and let the team work on it. If you hold back because you are shy or because you are uncomfortable holding your idea up to the scrutiny of the group, then you are shortchanging both yourself and the team. Trust yourself and trust that you are on the team for a reason—because you can contribute and provide helpful input.

8. Give ownership of great ideas to the team. Don't hog the limelight. Again, your team members won't forget. In fact, even if you came up with a specific idea, be willing to give the glory of the idea to the team. Your team-mates won't forget that you were willing to subsume your glory to the benefit of the entire group. Also, always keep in mind that there is no "I" in team. You are there to work as a group, and you should not be claiming credit that legitimately belongs to the team.

9. Talk to your coworkers. Don't just correspond electronically. I personally think there is no substitute for face-to-face discussions. You can read the other person's face as she is talking, which helps tremendously in understanding the subtext of the words she is speaking. If you find that your team is getting tied up in arguing about small issues or details, it may be because the team hasn't had enough personal meeting time to work out issues and clarify communication.

**10. However, virtual workspaces are a great way to share informa-
tion for teams that are geographically separated.** Google Docs is fast
becoming one of the most popular (and free) ways of sharing documents and
interacting about content. There are many other options in the marketplace,
both free and with a price tag.

**11. If there is an issue on the team, address it immediately. Don't let
it sit.** This is a good rule for any source of conflict. Address it as soon as possible so it doesn't fester. There may be a good reason for the conflict, such as a
basic disagreement about the direction of a project, and the sooner that issue
is articulated, the sooner it can be addressed. Don't be afraid of conflict. It is a
normal part of "teaming," and it is in the difference of opinions that you have
honest dialogue and the opportunity to take your teamwork to the next level.

12. Encourage creativity on your team. Be open to new and different
ideas. Encourage the team to brainstorm about different ways of approaching a project. Look at other industries to see if they provide learning for your
team. Talk to other staff and patrons at your library to see if ideas might
come from that direction. Don't forget that ideas can come from anywhere.

**13. Take the time at the end of a team project to review the work of
the team.** Many times at the end of a project, the team is tired from all the
work that has been done and just doesn't want to rehash everything. However,
it is in the rehashing that there is frequently opportunity for learning. You
aren't trying to get into "You should have done this," and "Boy, you messed
up by doing that." Rather, you are trying to identify how the team might have
worked together more effectively or reached a better end result by changing
certain behaviors or work processes. You want to ask how the next project
might be done better.

OTHER RESOURCES

Heathfield, Susan M. "Twelve Tips for Team Building: How to Build
   Successful Work Teams." http://humanresources.about.com/od/
   involvementteams/a/twelve_tip_team.htm.
   Useful article about how to build successful teams. Includes links to other sites

Team-building Leader.com. "Teambuilding Blog." www.teambuilding-leader
   .com/teambuilding-blog.html.
   A blog developed by a human resources professional that offers ideas for
   team-building activities

PART III | HELPFUL TO KNOW AS YOU
GAIN SOME EXPERIENCE

ELEVEN | PROMOTIONAL MARKETING

WHAT THIS CHAPTER IS ABOUT

Identifying the basics of marketing with a focus on how to do better promotional marketing at a library

WHY SHOULD YOU CARE?

As a librarian, you are very likely to do promotional marketing to encourage use of specific library products or services. This chapter will help you understand why marketing as a discipline is important to libraries and what to do to execute a marketing promotion effectively. However, it should be said that marketing is a very broad topic, with a much greater scope than I can cover in one chapter. If you are interested in marketing and would like to learn more about it, check out some of the additional resources listed at the end of the chapter.

THE HEART OF THE MATTER
What Is Marketing?

Marketing is a conversation between your library and anyone who might be interested in using your library. You tell potential users about the products and services that your library provides. You ask them to tell you what they like and dislike about those products and services, and then you adjust your offering to better provide what your users want. Marketing can happen for a specific product or service, or it can be done for an entire organization.

Marketing is composed of both planning and executing. At the planning stage you are defining what it is that you want to offer to your library users. You then develop a story that tells your users about the attributes of that offering. At the execution stage you tell that story to your users through advertising and promotion. After telling the story you ask your users what they think about your offering, collecting this information via market research. Once you receive input, you incorporate it into your planning, adjust your offering accordingly, and then go back and tell your new story.

Why Should Libraries Care about Marketing?

Libraries have a story to tell, both about their products and services and about their role in their communities. Marketing has been developed by the business world as an effective and efficient way of doing exactly that—telling a story about a product or service. It makes sense for libraries to appropriate this tool and use it to improve communications with their own users. If we don't clearly define who we are as organizations and the value that we can provide to the community through our products and services, then we risk losing our relevance in a world in which marketing is the norm rather than the exception.

What Are the Basic Components of Marketing?

Marketing strategy (the planning phase of marketing in which you develop your story) defines what makes your product or service or institution special. In other words, why should someone want what you have to offer? You are putting together a "story" for anyone who might be interested in your service, telling him what makes your service particularly appropriate in terms of meeting his needs. Telling that story in a short, compelling, succinct statement is called a *tagline*. Reflecting the story in a visual image is called a *logo*. Putting your tagline and visual image together is called a *brand*. A brand can be developed for a product, a service, or an institution.

Marketing tactics are the execution phase of marketing in which you tell your story to your audience and get feedback on that story. You can tell your story through various channels such as putting an ad in a newspaper or a magazine, or using your website. This is called advertising. You can also tell your story by talking about one specific product or service. This is called promotional marketing. Finally, after you've told your story, you'll want to ask for input from users and potential users as to what they thought about your story. This is called marketing research. There are many other elements of marketing (sales, website marketing, direct marketing, digital marketing) but these elements comprise marketing at its most basic level.

How Can a Library Improve Its Promotional Marketing?

Most libraries understand how to tell a story about an event. Week in and week out, libraries work to bring people in their doors to attend specific events. If you are new to a library you will learn this process very quickly. The following steps are provided as a quick methodology for creating an effective and efficient promotion for a library event:

Step 1: *Define your goal.* Before you start developing promotional or advertising materials, think first about what you are trying to accomplish. Are you trying to simply raise awareness about a specific event? Do you want people to take specific action as the result of your advertising? Do you want the reader to understand how this event fits into the library's role in the community? Do you only want to talk about the library's role in the community? Defining what you want the promotional piece to do will help you be clear about the story you are going to tell and to whom you are going to tell that story.

Step 2: *Define your audience.* Who are you talking to with this marketing piece? Librarians will tell you that they want to talk to "everyone." The only problem is that in order to talk to everyone effectively, you may have to tell several different stories several different ways. That results in clutter and confusion for the different audiences. Instead, think about the most important group to "hear" the story on any given promotional piece. Then phrase your story in such a way that it will be particularly relevant to your chosen audience. For example, if you have scheduled an author who writes books about how to potty train children, your audience is going to be parents, and your message should be phrased in such a way as to be accessible to that audience.

Step 3: *Identify your "story."* Before you develop advertising for a specific event, think carefully about your message. What is the most important point that you are trying to convey? In other words, what is your story? The most effective marketing piece has one clear message to it, not three or four or ten. All of us have seen cluttered web pages with so many messages on them that you can't figure out what to read first. That doesn't work. You have all of three or four seconds to capture the attention of a possible event attendee. You can only do that by telling one key story. Think about your story in a very visual way; the largest typeface on a web page or on a poster is going to be seen by viewers as the most important message, so make sure it is the most important message. Everything else that is provided in the way of information should be there to support your story, not tell another story.

Step 4: *Keep it simple, and use pictures instead of words whenever possible.* Keep in mind that visually, simpler is better. The window of opportunity to capture the attention of anyone looking at your marketing materials is very narrow. Don't make the viewer work hard at figuring out what you are saying. Someone once told me that the secret to a good presentation was to be brief, be bold, and be gone. I think the same holds true with promotional marketing. There is always the desire to add one more piece of information. Don't give in to that temptation! Think about using pictures instead of words if you can find pictures to tell your story. Yes, it is trite, but a picture *is* worth a thousand words. People will stop to look at a picture but might never stop to read a poster or flyer.

The Power of Pictures in Promotion

Recently the library at which I am the director held a Community Day for emergency preparedness. The two staff members who put together the promotional materials included a big picture of a dog on the poster promoting the event. When I first saw the poster, I stopped and did a double take. (I'm a dog lover, so naturally the dog picture caught my attention.) I asked my colleagues why the dog was on the poster. Their answer was a perfect demonstration of keeping promotional materials simple but effective: part of emergency preparations in any community involves getting animal owners to put together emergency kits not just for themselves but also for their pets. The local humane society would be at the Community Day to talk about this. The two smart staff members realized that a picture of a dog on a poster would capture the attention of an animal-lover (as it did with me), so the picture of a dog was actually a great way to increase awareness about the event among the target audience.

Step 5: *Keep it consistent.* As you develop promotional pieces for events at your library, think about the "look" that you are conveying. If you put all the pieces together for a year of events, would you know that all those events were held at the same library? Start thinking about how you can be consistent in certain elements of your promotional pieces (Using the same colors? Always putting the library's logo in the same place on promotional pieces?) so that after a period of time, anyone looking at the materials will start to recognize them as coming from your library. This is a good thing because it simplifies the communication process. People immediately understand where the communication comes from, along with all the inherent concepts contained therein (it comes from the library, the library is a trusted source of information, I like the library, etc.) and they don't have to think too hard about the information being conveyed. In today's world of instantaneous communication, if you make someone work too hard to get your message, you will lose him.

Step 6: *Use your promotional marketing to talk to people outside your normal audience.* Putting posters up in your library about an event is important because regular library users will see the information and be made aware of the event. However, don't forget to "talk" about events outside the library. Think about where you might find your target audience in your community and then make sure you put your marketing promotions in those places. For example, going back to the potty-training event, don't forget to put posters at local daycare centers, Gymborees, other libraries in the area, and local pediatricians' offices. Generally, all of those places are more than willing to help a library promote an event.

Step 7: *Ask for feedback.* Don't forget to ask for input after you've held an event at your library. Put surveys out at programs or hand them out at the

Reaching Outside Audiences

A staff member at my library took the time to map out all of the places in town that are willing to put up posters for the library. Whenever the library has a special event, we have a special volunteer whose only job is to walk around town and put up posters in all of those locations. Our volunteer loves this job, and is incredibly helpful to the library's promotional marketing efforts in reaching individuals outside our normal patron base when they are our target audience.

door as people come into your meeting room. Use the survey to ask how they found out about the event, listing all of the marketing promotions that you used. That will help you understand if your marketing promotions are effective. Ask if they liked the event and if they thought the content was appropriate for them. That will help you figure out if you've targeted the right audience for the program. Asking for this type of feedback will also help you determine what you might do differently both in terms of choosing the event to have and how you promote it.

Example of a Post-Event Survey

Thank you for attending today's event at the library. It would be helpful to future event planning if you could answer the following four questions for us. Please either leave this survey on your chair when you leave or hand it to any staff member.

1. How did you hear about today's event? (Check as many as apply.)
   - ❑ Newspaper article
   - ❑ E-mail announcement from the library
   - ❑ Poster about the event in town
   - ❑ Poster about the event at the library
   - ❑ Heard about it from a friend or family member
   - ❑ Saw it on the town calendar
   - ❑ Other (please identify)

2. Please rate the degree to which you enjoyed the event on a scale of 1 to 5. (1 = did not enjoy at all, 5 = greatly enjoyed the event)
   1   2   3   4   5

3. Please rate the degree to which the event met your expectations on a scale of 1 to 5. (1 = did not meet my expectations at all, 5 = perfectly met my expectations)
   1   2   3   4   5

4. Please give us any other feedback you might have about the event. Thank you for your help!

OTHER RESOURCES

Carmichael, Evan. "The Top 50 Marketing Blogs to Watch in 2009." www
.evancarmichael.com/Tools/Top-50-Marketing-Blogs-To-Watch-In-2009
.htm.
Contains a nice list of 2009 influential marketing blogs

Doucett, Elisabeth. *Creating Your Library Brand: Communicating Your
Relevance and Value to Your Patrons.* Chicago: American Library
Association, 2008.
OK, I'm tooting my own horn here, but if you are interested in turning your
library into a brand (and obviously I recommend that) then this is a simple,
easy-to-understand methodology for doing that.

Duct Tape Marketing. www.ducttapemarketing.com/blog.
Oriented to small businesses. I like it because it has a lot of free content and
the methodology used to market small businesses is very similar to many of
the ways to market a library.

Kotler, Philip. *Marketing Insights from A to Z: 80 Concepts Every Manager Needs
to Know.* Hoboken, NJ: John Wiley and Sons, 2003.
You can't go wrong reading anything about marketing that is written by Phil
Kotler. He is the guru of marketing. I like this book because the information
is easily accessible.

Kotler, Philip, and Gary Armstrong. *Principles of Marketing.* Upper Saddle
River, NJ: Prentice Hall, 2001.
Again, you can never go wrong with Phil Kotler. This is a serious book and is
meant for those who really want to make a study of marketing.

MarketingProfs. www.marketingprofs.com.
One of my favorites because it takes a teaching perspective toward marketing.
It has some free content, or you can pay to upgrade to premium.

MarketingSherpa. "SherpaBlog." www.marketingsherpa.com/sherpablog
.html.
Another one of my favorites. Simple to understand, easy to follow

| TWELVE | **THINKING LIKE A RETAILER** |

WHAT THIS CHAPTER IS ABOUT

Identifying what librarians can learn from the art of retailing

WHY SHOULD YOU CARE?

Retail stores live or die based on how many people walk in the door. Retailers have spent years identifying ways of bringing more people into their stores. As a librarian, don't you also want to bring as many people as possible through your library's doors?

THE HEART OF THE MATTER

Successful retailers are experts in getting people in their doors and enticing them to purchase objects in their stores. The following is a brief summary of some of the ways in which retailers do their job and some of the potential implications for librarians who are working to bring more people into their library—and, once they are in the library, using more of the services that libraries provide.

Lesson 1: *Location, location, location.* Retailers have learned well from the real estate business. They look at each location inside their store as real estate, with some locations being very valuable and others less so. They put their most attractive, compelling products in the best locations, where store visitors will see the products. In grocery stores this generally means putting produce or the bakery right by the front door. People smell the wonderful odor of baking bread and want to buy some. Or they see the beautiful colors and shapes of fresh fruit and vegetables and want to buy them. Incidentally, both of these food categories provide high profits to the store. The products that are less compelling (and have a lower profit margin) are usually found in the center aisles of any grocery store. In many grocery stores, the products needed most regularly (such as eggs and milk) are found in the farthest aisle of the store, forcing the shopper to walk through the entire store before they find the product they need. While this is a very annoying practice for us shoppers, it makes sense if you consider it from the retailers' perspective: profit.

The learning that libraries can get from this retailing practice is simple. The library has many pieces of indoor real estate, some locations being more valuable than others. A smart librarian will review the real estate in a department to determine what are the most "valuable" areas (where people spend a lot of time and are likely to notice particular displays), and what are the less important areas (the back of stacks, in dark areas). You can figure this out the same way retailers do, although you probably already have a good sense

First Impressions

This is a fun exercise. The next time you go grocery shopping, pay attention to the first impression you get when you walk into your grocery store. Do you see beautiful displays of produce or smell flowers or baking bread? Whatever it is, it is likely to be (a) enjoyable for you, and (b) profitable for the store. After you've done this in a grocery store, try the same thing when you walk into your library. What is the first thing that strikes your senses? Do you see smiling faces and a clean building? Do you see messy bulletin boards and book displays that have big gaps in them? Consider that a welcoming presence is just as important in a library as a grocery store!

of what is and isn't valuable space. Put out displays in various areas of your department. Spend some time every day watching and counting how many people walk by the display and how many stop and look at the display. When there are a lot of people stopping to look at books or movies or CDs in a particular area, that is probably valuable real estate. Another way to figure out valuable real estate is to watch and notice where people first stop when they walk into your area of the library. Those places are also valuable locations.

The same lesson can be applied to your library's website. The website also has valuable and less valuable real estate, and careful consideration should be given to what information goes in each area. Obviously your most important items should go on your home page. Keep the most important of these items "above the fold" on the website so that readers don't have to scroll down to find it. After your home page, the next most valuable real estate locations are the main navigation pages. Think carefully about what goes on each of those pages and make sure that you keep that information up-to-date and relevant.

Lesson 2: *Put the books where they can be seen—easily.* Retailers make it easy to find big-selling items. For example, grocery stores put the biggest sellers at eye level, and less important products go on higher and lower shelves. Walk down the cookie aisle, the coffee aisle, or the cereal aisle. You'll always see the big brands that you immediately recognize at eye level, and you can be guaranteed that the products at that level are the best sellers for the grocery store. In fact grocery stores hire people whose entire jobs are composed of evaluating the placement of products on shelves based on profitability.

The same idea applies to library shelves. Don't put displays of books down too low or up too high. Make sure they are approximately at eye level so that your library patrons will see the materials on display quickly and easily. Put the best sellers where everyone will see them. If you would like specific titles to be noticed quickly, put them at eye level. Don't make your patrons bend

Location, Location, Location

Don't make the mistake of thinking that just because you've always had displays in a specific location, that location constitutes valuable real estate. Displays may have started going up in a specific location because there was a bookshelf sitting there, or the light was good for reading, or there was no other location for a display. Try different places in the library that have never had displays and see if they garner more or less attention than the old standby locations.

over to scan titles on lower shelves. Unless they are looking for a specific title, they won't do it (or they might do it but will complain the entire way!).

Lesson 3: *Being a neatnik librarian is a good thing.* Retailers work constantly to keep their shelves well stocked and neat. Every evening after closing, staff generally goes through a store and neatens up shelves and racks, a practice called "facing out." Given that the shelves will be messy ten minutes after the first customer walks in the store, why do they bother? Because customers are much more drawn to investigate a clean, neat shelf than they are to go rooting around on a messy shelf, searching out what they want. Grocery stores have learned well not make their customers work too hard.

The implication for a librarian is straightforward. At the end of the work period, spending just a few minutes walking through an area and picking it up will make a world of difference to your library's patrons and to your fellow librarians. Put books back on shelves and push unused chairs under tables. Move magazines and newspapers back to their racks. Make sure the shelves are free of dust. This picking up is a good practice partly because it makes life easier for the next librarian working. However, there are other benefits. A neat section is inviting. Your library patrons will be comfortable walking into an area that is obviously well maintained. They will be able to find what they want easily, and that is just as critical in a library as in a grocery store.

Additionally, if you work in a public library it is important to show that you are taking good care of the materials and resources paid for by the taxpayer. This reduces the likelihood that anyone in the library will feel comfortable trashing the environment. It is the same theory used in big cities on subway systems. Graffiti is never allowed to sit on a train, because if it does it indicates that no one is watching or cares about the state of the train. That subsequently sends out the signal that it is OK to continue putting graffiti on trains, and soon the trains are covered. Libraries work the same way: if you maintain them regularly, it is much more likely that users will treat the library building with the same level of respect.

Lesson 4: *Get those "slow sellers" out where people can see them.* When retailers want to sell a lot of any particular product, they put it on display shelves at the ends of aisles. Ends of aisles are considered to be valuable real estate. People notice what is on the end of an aisle, whether they are shopping every aisle in the store or just the perimeter. Big companies spend huge amounts of money "buying" the end-of-aisle space from grocery stores so they can display their products, knowing that they will more than make their money back in the form of additional products sold.

Libraries are set up in much the same way as retail stores. People generally walk around the edges of the building and go into the stacks only for a specific need or if something catches their eye. If you start putting displays at the end of the aisles in your library, it is almost guaranteed that people will stop and notice. This is also an excellent technique for pulling people into your stacks so they will look at all those wonderful (and mostly forgotten) books in your stacks. However, a word of caution is in order here: end-of-aisle displays get noticed for a very short period of time, and then they fade into the background. Therefore, end-of-aisle displays need to change regularly (as often as one to two weeks) to keep people coming back for more information. If you can keep up that schedule, people will start seeing the end-of-aisle displays as destinations of choice versus happenstance. They will seek out the displays regularly—and that's the kind of behavior that helps drive up your circulation statistics.

Lesson 5: *If no one reads a book, get rid of it.* Retailers constantly assess and reassess how products are selling in their stores. If a product doesn't sell, it is taken off the shelves or moved to a less valuable location.

This lesson is most relevant for public librarians. For the most part, if a book doesn't circulate, then the librarian in that department needs to make an effort to get the book out of the stacks and see if the public still has any interest in the book. If the book still doesn't circulate, then it needs to be weeded out of the collection. Weeding needs to be an ongoing process that never stops, because the public's interest in specific topics changes constantly and we need to react to (or even anticipate) those changes.

Lesson 6: *Understand how your library is used.* Retailers analyze very carefully the "purchase cycle" of products. This means they know how often the average consumer comes to the store to buy a particular product. They also pay close attention to the "grocery basket" or items purchased by the average consumer. They understand that if a customer buys milk, she generally also buys other staples such as eggs and bread. The learning from that is that if one of those products is on sale, you don't need to put the other two on sale; they will get picked up by the shopper anyway.

The learning from this is to understand what your library users want and what they use in your library. If you are in an academic library, you need to have a collection that supports the curriculum of your school. If you are in a public library or a special library, then you need to have the books and materials that people want and will use. Understand which parts of your collection are heavily used and which parts are not. If a specific section is not used, see if you can build some interest in it by putting books out on display. If your circulation system allows it, get monthly updates on how many books are moving from specific parts of your collection. Compare those numbers to the same period a year ago and two years ago. Have there been any major changes up or down? If you put books out on display about one topic, is it likely to drive interest in another topic? The key here is to be aware that you can learn a great deal about what your library users want by understanding how they use the library.

Lesson 7: *Appearances do matter.* Retailers know that how a product looks plays an important role in attracting the attention of potential buyers. Packaging is seen as being almost as important as the actual product itself in terms of its ability to influence someone into buying it. While you might not agree with that perspective (think about all the wasteful packaging in the world), it does get across the idea that appearances do matter.

The learning from this lesson is also very direct. Look at the books, DVDs, CDs, newspapers, and magazines in your collection. Are your books clean and neat (covers not ripped, no writing inside them, older books weeded)? Bottom line: people don't want to take out materials from your library if they are old and ratty looking. While a librarian might look at a tired book and think, "Wow, a lot of people have read and enjoyed that book!" a library user will probably look at it and think, "Yuck, that looks old and dirty." Take care of your collection. If you don't have the budget to put new covers on books when they get heavily used, you can certainly make a point of keeping materials clean and in good repair. Seek out volunteers in your community who might be willing to help keep materials clean on a regular basis if you don't have enough staff to manage this task. It will be worth the effort.

Lesson 8: *Talk regularly with your library users.* Retailers know their customers. They know what their customers buy most regularly; they want what catches the interest of their customers; and they talk to their customers whenever possible to understand what they want. A good retailer knows her regular users, and she will work hard to develop a personal relationship with that individual, knowing that everyone would rather do business with a friend than a stranger.

Most librarians know this lesson well. They need to maintain a constant conversation with their library users to understand what their customers want. If you recommend a book to a patron, the next time you see him, ask what he thought of the book. If you helped a student find a resource for a paper, ask how the paper was received by her professor. Librarians are in the service business, but we do need to make sure we are providing the right service.

In this chapter I've focused on what librarians can learn from grocery retailers. However, there are equally as many lessons to be learned from other types of retailers in the marketplace today: department stores, clothing stores, the big box stores like Walmart, etc. Just pay attention as you do your weekly shopping and you'll find some good ideas that might be useful in your library.

OTHER RESOURCES

Falk, Edgar A. *1,001 Ideas to Create Retail Excitement,* revised edition. New York: Prentice Hall, 2003.
> This book provides basic retail merchandising concepts. It will be useful to librarians who are newcomers to the concepts of retailing.

Progressive Grocer. www.progressivegrocer.com.
> I like this magazine because it regularly talks about what is new and cutting-edge in the grocery industry, and that's where I get ideas for the library. There is a yearly cost for the magazine, but you can get some free content online.

Editors of VM+SD, *Visual Merchandising 5*. Cincinnati, OH: Media Group International, 2007.
> A great deal of merchandising is based around visual appeal. This book gives you the pictures and the ideas about new ways of presenting materials to your public. If Edgar Falk's book is for retail beginners, this book is for those willing to push the envelope and try new ideas.

THIRTEEN | STRATEGIC PLANNING

WHAT THIS CHAPTER IS ABOUT

Defining what strategic planning is and demonstrating how it is important to every staff person in a library, regardless of her position

WHY SHOULD YOU CARE?

Your library's strategic plan defines how the library is planning to evolve and change over the next one to five years (the length of most strategic plans today). If you understand how strategic planning is done and know where your library is heading, you can decide if and how you want to be part of that change. A library's strategy is critical in helping you define your own career plan.

THE HEART OF THE MATTER

Strategy is actually quite simple and does not have to be a two-year, arduous journey of work that everyone hates. The best library strategic plan that I have seen to date was produced by the Chicago Public Library (www.chipublib .org/aboutcpl/cpl2010/index.php). It is simple, short, and straightforward. I would guess that a lot of work went into the final document, and the end result is a model of simplicity and elegance that I'm guessing is used by the library on a regular basis. In any case, this is a great example of how strategic planning can turn out for every library.

The process used in strategic planning is linear and simple: a strategic planning team identifies the state of the library today. Then they determine where the organization should be in three to five years. Finally, they figure out what they have to do to move the library from where it is today to where they want to be in the future. That, in a nutshell, is strategic planning at its simplest level.

A strategic planning team generally includes key decision makers and stakeholders in the library. In a public library this might include the library director, the president of the library board, the head of the Friends of the Library, senior staff members, and individuals from the community. In an academic library it would include the library director, senior staff, possibly one or two faculty and key administrators who have an impact on the library, and some representation from the student population. Generally, a strategic planning team is somewhere between six and ten individuals, although the team can be larger if the individual running the planning process has experience with managing large teams. A good rule of thumb is the larger the team, the longer the work takes to get done.

A strategic planning team starts by evaluating its library in three ways. Together, these analyses are called a situational assessment:

1. They assess the library in relationship to their own definition of success. (We want to increase the number of new library users by 10 percent in this fiscal year.)

2. Then the team evaluates the library in relationship to similar libraries (comparing an academic library to a similar academic library).

3. Finally, the team assesses the library in the context of its environment. (What role does a public library play in its city? What is happening in the city, county, and state that might have an effect on the library?)

Tools Used in a Situational Assessment

Assessing the Library

Number of visitors through the door

Circulation of materials

Number of programs and participants

Assessing the Library Compared to Other Libraries

Generally the same factors are used as in the library's self-assessment, but the measures are compared to the same measures in other, similar libraries.

Assessing the Library within the Community

Surveys done with library users to gauge their general satisfaction with the library's services, likes/dislikes about specific services, awareness of programs or opportunities at the library, what they would like to see change at the library

Surveys done with nonusers to gauge why don't they use the library, what would it take to get them more involved with the library

Feedback from key stakeholders in the library's community. In an academic library this would include faculty; in a public library it would include members of the library's Friends organization or members of the board of trustees.

Key trends in the environment that could have an impact on the library. For a public library this could include changes in demographics, economics, and local businesses. For an academic library it might include changes in enrollment, building programs on campus, and the economic status of the campus.

Once the situational assessment is complete, how does the strategic planning team review the information? They start by evaluating each piece of data in the assessment item by item, and determining the learning or implication from that information. If they review the assessment and discover that the library put a new teaching program in place and usage of reference materials immediately increased, then the implication might be that participants in the program quickly learned the importance of the reference materials in relationship to the class curriculum. If the team can't figure out any implications from a specific component of the assessment, then they generally get rid of that data. Data is useful only so far as it provides learning about the library.

After the team has reviewed the assessment and determined the implications, they will go back through the assessment a second time, looking at the implications identified in the first go-through. The team will work to determine if the implication identifies a *strength* of the library, a *weakness* of the library, an *opportunity* in the environment for the library, or a *threat* in the environment to the library. This is what is generally referred to as a SWOT analysis. A SWOT analysis will essentially define the state of the library today.

Just the Facts

A SWOT analysis is only as effective or useful as the situation assessment from which it is derived. Some strategic planning teams simply list out what they see as an organization's strengths, weaknesses, opportunities, and threats. That misses the whole point of doing a SWOT. A SWOT should be derived from *facts and data*, not from what someone thinks or guesses at. The materials collected in the situation assessment are the facts that should drive the SWOT. Each fact collected should be a strength, weakness, opportunity, or threat. If a fact does not fall into one of these categories, then it is not important enough to be included in the situation assessment.

At this point in the strategic planning process, the strategic planning team should be able to write its library's mission. A mission defines what the library seeks to provide to its community today. It is a way of informing its users what the library aspires to do every day, how the library does that, and what it is the library is trying to achieve by doing that work. A mission statement should be short, concise, and to the point. (See box for some examples of mission statements.) When the strategic planning team has completed the mission statement, everyone in the library should at least be able to articulate

Does It Matter?

Another way of reviewing data and determining implications is for the team to look at the data and say, "Why does it matter?" If they can't answer that question, then they know the data is not proving informative and can be eliminated.

the portion of the statement that identifies what the library seeks to do. If no one in the library can articulate that, then the mission statement isn't short enough or relevant enough.

Once the team has defined the state of the library today, they will work to determine where they want the library to be in the future. This part of strategic planning is about creating a vision. There is no right or wrong answer in creating a vision. Rather, a vision statement identifies what the strategic

More on Mission Statements

A mission statement is the declaration of the "work of the organization today." It is meant to define what business an organization is in. A mission statement often (but not always) has the following format:

The mission of Library X is:

To enrich the quality of life in our community (what the library does)

By providing information and ideas (how the library does it)

That educate, enrich, inspire, and entertain (what the library seeks to achieve with what it does)

Examples of mission statements

Arby's Restaurants: "To provide an exceptional dining experience that satisfies our guests' grown-up tastes by being a 'Cut-Above' in everything we do."

New York Public Library: "The mission of The New York Public Library is to use its available resources in a balanced program of collecting, cataloging, and conserving books and other materials, and providing ready access directly to individual library users and to users elsewhere through cooperating libraries and library networks. The New York Public Library's responsibility is to serve as a great storehouse of knowledge at the heart of one of the world's information centers, and to function as an integral part of a fabric of information and learning that stretches across the nation and the world."

Smith College: "Smith College educates women of promise for lives of distinction. A college of and for the world, Smith links the power of the liberal arts to excellence in research and scholarship, developing leaders for society's challenges."

planning team believes are smart goals for the library over the long term. Sometimes vision statements are very large, sweeping expressions of the organization's focus, such as "XYZ seeks to become the best provider of car materials in the world." Sometimes vision statements are smaller in scope. (See box for some examples.)

How does the team go about defining a vision for the library? They start by looking at where their community (whether that be a town, a university, or a business) is heading. They can do this by reviewing the strategic planning documents of their community. The next step is to determine what needs the library *could* fulfill in that future vision of the community. They then review those potential roles and determine which ones the library *should* own. Sometimes the library might identify four or five different roles it could take on in the future, but it might not make sense for the library to own all of those roles because of funding issues or inadequate staffing or expertise. Or there might be another organization in the community better suited to take on that role. All of this is part of the discussion that a strategic planning team will go through. Once they determine the role or roles they think the library should own, then they have the basic components of their vision statement.

The library now has a clear understanding of where it is and where it wants to go. The final part of the strategic planning process is for the team to determine what actions the library will need to take to move from the present to the future. The simplest way of doing this is for the team to review their SWOT analysis one more time to assess each strength, weakness, opportunity, and threat. They determine if they want to maintain a strength, if they want to address or fix a weakness, if they want to take advantage of an opportunity, and if they want to buttress the library against potential threats. Once

More on Vision Statements

A vision statement should be an exciting declaration of where an organization wants to be in the future. It is the goal that the organization is seeking to reach. Here are three examples of vision statements:

- "No child in our city will go to bed hungry." (soup kitchen)
- "In two decades, our services will no longer be needed." (literacy program)
- "We will be recognized as the best symphony orchestra in America." (symphony orchestra)

they determine this, they have the core components of their plan for moving forward.

In many libraries the final step in this process is to do a yearly action plan. An action plan is simply the identification of what will be accomplished that year in terms of moving the organization toward its vision. One reason a library has action plans is to ensure it is keeping a focus on the strategic plan and that all parts of the library are moving forward toward the same goal.

Generally, strategic planning is done at a senior level. This may result in newer staff members assuming it has no relevance to them. But although a new or more junior staff member might not be directly involved in strategic planning, it still has tremendous importance to her. What if a strategic plan says that a public library is going to focus heavily on the development of services to the community's growing senior population—but you've just been hired to run teen services? You need to know that's the future direction of the library, and you need to define what your role will be in that process. I would suggest that anyone being hired at a library ask to see the library's strategic plan before accepting a job. Otherwise, you might find that you are in for some interesting surprises a year or two down the road, as products and services change in accordance with the library's strategic plan. If you are aware of the library's direction, then you can more proactively determine your role in that direction. Don't stick your head in the sand, say, "It isn't part of my responsibilities," and then be surprised when "stuff" happens. Get involved, understand the direction of the library, and then ask questions about your role in that direction.

OTHER RESOURCES

McNamara, Carter. "Strategic Planning (In Nonprofit or For-profit Organizations)." http://managementhelp.org/plan_dec/str_plan/str _plan.htm.
A good in-depth article about how to approach strategic planning for nonprofit organizations. This article also includes a list of recommended books to help do strategic planning at a nonprofit.

Nelson, Sandra. *The New Planning for Results: A Streamlined Approach.* Chicago: American Library Association, 2001.
This is a very helpful book and is the standard for public libraries to use for guidance in strategic planning. I adjust and shorten the process outlined here to better meet the individual needs of my library.

FOURTEEN | **TREND TRACKING**

WHAT THIS CHAPTER IS ABOUT

Finding and analyzing trends that could have implications for your library

WHY SHOULD YOU CARE?

In the Internet age, the relevancy of libraries is often questioned, because "everything can be found for free on the Internet." One of the best ways to remain relevant is to have a clear understanding of where the world is going and to determine a role for the library in that new world. But you can't do this if you don't understand new directions, new trends, and new ideas. This chapter is about how you can surf that wave of information to ensure that you are pulling out the best ideas to use in your library and in your job.

THE HEART OF THE MATTER

A quick definition of trends and fads will be helpful at this point. Fads are ideas that sweep through portions of our society, have a short-term impact, and are gone, leaving few ripples behind. Pet rocks were a fad. Trends may start as fads, but somewhere along the way they turn into concepts that have more staying power. A trend is a concept that can have real impact on our lives and our society. A trend more often than not will enter into the mainstream of society and have an impact on multiple levels of the society (including libraries). Therefore, what we are discussing here is trends, not fads.

Trend tracking is fun. And because it is fun, sometimes I view it as more of a luxury than a "have-to-do." Don't make that mistake. If librarians are not aware of, or are behind the curve in understanding and taking advantage of, today's trends, then we all run the risk of becoming irrelevant and unimportant to our society. Pursuing every trend is not the objective of this process. Rather, your goal is to learn how to identify *and evaluate* trends for any implications they might have for your library. Once you can do that, then you can decide if you want to jump on a specific trend or leave it for someone else.

The following process will help you pursue the goal of learning how to identify trends and determine their implications for your library.

Step 1: *Identify potential sources of information for societal and library trend tracking.* Trend tracking is now an entire profession in the world of business. There are people and companies that focus exclusively on tracking trends and defining their potential implications for businesses. Because this is a relatively new phenomenon, most of these trend trackers are Internet-centered. They tend to share their information broadly and freely on the Internet with the goal of attracting business to them. This means that librarians can find a tremendous amount of trend-tracking information online, for free.

Go online and search for "trend tracking" or "cool hunting." You'll get a whole list of individuals and organizations that do this; in fact, you may be somewhat overwhelmed by the options. (I'm including my list of resources to help with that.) You need to do some evaluation of the websites you've found to determine which ones will be useful and provide good information. I would look for sites that (1) have been in existence for more than ten minutes, (2) have received positive reviews in either well-known marketing or advertising journals (the equivalent of peer review in the world of marketing), and (3) provide a great deal of free information—otherwise, what's the point? I generally try to find sites that provide general rather than specific information. For example, I'm less interested in specific trends in the car industry,

Trend-Tracking Sources

These are some websites I visit to collect trend information, and why I like each one:

www.trendwatching.com–Trends identified by a network of "trend spotters" around the world. Useful because it conceptualizes trends for you and provides examples of how the trend is demonstrated. Lots of content for free. Easy to read and access the concepts

www.coolhunting.com–Identifies "cool stuff" going on in the world across many, many categories of possible interest such as art, books, green, and housewares. This site does less trend identification work for you, but it is a great source of ideas if you are comfortable extrapolating trends out of current happenings.

www.thecoolhunter.net–This blog is similar to coolhunting.com in that it identifies ideas in many different categories. Somewhat edgier in content with a very strong art/design perspective. It is particularly useful for tracking "cool" events that might provide ideas for library events.

www.ted.com–This site provides audio feed for "riveting talks by inspiring people." The TED site bills itself as in the business of spreading ideas. You won't find trends identified, but what you will find are the big ideas that could turn into the trends of tomorrow. The site has a global perspective, which helps makes it intriguing.

www.tomorrowstrends.com–This is a blog that "tracks what's new and what's next. It covers the areas of business innovation, design, technology, and societal trends." The site compiles information around various topics. I like it because it crosses from business to entertainment to science and doesn't just focus on one area.

www.trendhunter.com–This is the most expansive trend-hunting site that I use. It has a huge amount of content about innovation in multiple fields. It can be a bit overwhelming because there is so much information. However, its depth makes it a great resource for identifying multiple trend ideas. It includes a great page with "Top Sites for Trend Spotting and Cool Hunting" at www.trendhunter .com/topsites.

www.google.com/trends–This is an interesting site with which to experiment. You type in a search term and the trends tool will track

(CONT.)

Trend-Tracking Sources (cont.)

on a graph the average worldwide traffic in that search term. The site is primarily useful because it can show you if searches on a specific term are increasing, thereby indicating greater awareness and the development of a potential trend.

www.google.com/insights/search–This site aims to "provide insight into broad search terms." Typing in a search term will provide you with search interest over time, regional interest, top searches that relate to your search, and rising searches related to your search. This site is probably most useful in providing other search topics that might be related to your trend search.

but I'm very interested in trends toward appreciation of the baby boomers in marketing. The more general the trends, the easier it is for me to determine its implications for what I do in the library. At this point, I'm also looking for articles that have already identified trends for me. I'm not doing any trend determination on my own, because that takes a lot more time.

Step 2: *Develop a method for regularly reviewing those resources.* I block out an hour every Friday morning to sit down and go through my trend tracking. I try to hold that hour on my schedule, no matter what. I start by going through the new information on each site, scanning for content that grabs my attention. If something is particularly interesting or seems like it could have direct and immediate relevance to the library, I'll do some additional, general searches on my own through common business resources (www.adage.com, www.businessweek.com, Business Source Premier) to see if I can find more information. I spend a total of about twenty minutes reviewing, reading, and researching, and then I write down each idea in two to three words (to be used in the next step), along with a few additional sentences to summarize the basic concept and the source for that information. (I always track this so that if I need to refer back to the source I know where to find it quickly.) I usually spend about ten minutes doing this, so I don't spend more than two or three minutes per idea that I discover. If I come up with ten ideas in a session, I'm very happy.

Step 3: *Search social networking sites.* I spend another ten minutes using the two to three keywords I identified above to search social network sites such as Twitter and Facebook to see if anything of interest pops up. Sometimes

Applying Trends: Sample Idea List

Ideas from trend watching and possible translation to my library, July 6, 2009:

"Forever beta"—putting out less-than-perfect ideas, programs and asking for input so that they can evolve and improve (trendwatching.com)
- Try more ideas in the library. Ask for feedback. Evolve and change on the fly. If an idea doesn't work, don't be afraid to toss it out and try something else.

Pop-up restaurants and stores (trendwatching.com)
- Why not have a pop-up event in the library lobby regularly with downtown restaurants and stores? Restaurants could provide food samples and info about their restaurants, library patrons could sample food, and library would be having fun/interesting/free events going on.

An airline for pets (coolbusinessideas.com)
- Could we have a "pet day" or "pet morning" at the library when people could bring in their dogs when they come to the library?

Farm stays becoming a hit (coolbusinessideas.com)
- How about having a library open house at which people can try out a librarian's job? Or they can have a special "before the library is opened tour"?

Testimonials from actual clients
- How about asking library visitors to give us testimonials? On video? Or in writing? Would they be willing to pay more in taxes to fund library services?

Word of mouth marketing works best (coolbusinessideas.com)
- Could we have a "refer a friend day" at the library? Ask every library patron to bring in one friend to get a library card?

Sainsbury's grocery stores using plates in their parking lots to generate enough energy to help run the stores (coolbusinessideas .com)
- Could you do the same thing at the library but have the energy generation come through the foot traffic of people going into the library?

Stylish Band-Aids (coolhunter.com)
- How about a program where kids can design their own library card?

Rooftop films/summer outdoor films/mobile movies (coolhunter.com)
- How about a summer film series in the garden? Or sponsored by the library but held by the gazebo?

you can find a great Facebook site of someone who is driving a trend or who is a "trend groupie," and he can prove to be a mine of information around the concept. Don't spend a huge amount of time doing this, but it can be a helpful way of amplifying an idea that you might be developing. However, don't forget that you are trying to identify trend possibilities as much as existing trends. Therefore, the ideas you are researching may only be at a very nascent stage.

Step 4: *Review each idea that you pulled out of your research, considering potential implications for your library.* Don't be afraid at this point to be a little crazy and to have some fun. This is really the brainstorming part of this enterprise, and as we always say when brainstorming, there are no bad ideas. Go through all of the ideas that you captured in your scanning. Ask yourself how this trend might be relevant to your library or your job. Jot down anything that comes to mind. Trust your intuition and write down the first ideas that come to mind. Write down questions about the idea. Don't worry if the idea seems crazy or too vague. All you are doing here is getting ideas out of your brain and onto paper. If nothing comes to mind, then there might not be any value in this trend for your library, so move on to the next one. This idea should be fairly fluid and fun. If you can find a fellow librarian to do this with, it is even more interesting because you will find that you start to build on each other's ideas. This brainstorming phase should take about twenty minutes. When you have completed this work, stop and put your idea list in a file.

Step 5: *Leave your idea list in a file until you start the same process the next week.* I firmly believe that good ideas get better after "percolating." Let them sit and allow your subconscious to noodle them. Then for the first ten minutes of your next trend-tracking hour, before you start scanning your resources for new idea leads, look at what you wrote down the prior week. Can you expand on any of the ideas? Do any of the ideas lead you in a new direction? Did you find any information during the week that might lead you to think an idea was potentially very good or very bad? Go through your list and amend it, based on this process. Each week during these ten-minute scans, review and edit the prior weeks' lists. After a period of time (it could be a week or two or three) you'll find that certain ideas hold up to scrutiny and keep growing in interest. Those are the ideas that should take the forefront for actual development. I generally don't let an idea sit for more than six weeks without moving it to the next step. Otherwise, it is too easy to miss a trend opportunity.

Step 6: *When you identify the ideas that you want to pursue for your library, get together with some of your fellow librarians to help you review the ideas and find the good and bad about them.* You might ask an informal group to meet for a brown-bag lunch and discussion session, or do it after work over a dinner out. Share one of the ideas that has worked its way to the top of your file. Ask them to first see if there is any way they could amplify or build on the idea. Would the idea be useful to them individually in their section of the library? Does the idea intrigue them, or do they immediately brush it off? Work to find reasons to try ideas rather than identify all the problems with implementing something. Once you've gone through the brainstorming discussion, ask them to tell you all the reasons why the idea won't work. Try hard to poke holes in the idea. Find all the reasons for failure and write them down. Put together a list of the pros and cons that you've developed. Ideally, the pros will outweigh the cons—but they might not. That's OK. Don't discard anything yet, but go on to the next step.

Step 7: *Put the ideas back in the file and let them sit for another week.* They need to percolate again. Pull the ideas out one more time at the end of the week. If an idea still seems intriguing, start pursuing it even if it has a big list of cons against it. At least now you should have a clear list of issues that you can address as you plan how to move the idea forward. If the pros of the idea are lengthy, then you are in even better shape to move the idea into development.

Step 8: *Once a month, pull out one idea that has gone through steps 1–7.* Spend an additional hour writing a one-page summary of why your library should give that idea a try. The summary should never be longer than one page, and here's why: you are going to use this summary to "sell" your manager (or the library director or the board of trustees) on pursuing this idea. The following are the key elements to include in this summary:

- *Summary of project idea:* One or two sentences outlining what the idea is
- *Sources:* How did this idea surface? You don't need an in-depth bibliography here. You just want to demonstrate that you have done some real research and this is an honest idea floating in the marketplace, not something you just dreamed up.
- *Value to the library:* If this idea is implemented, what could it do for your library?
- *Cost:* How much would it cost to implement this idea? This doesn't have to be exact information, but you should have some sense if

Sample of Request for Project Consideration

Summary of project idea
Develop "Refer a Friend Day" at Curtis Memorial Library. Ask every Curtis user to bring a friend without a library card to the library on Monday, January 22. The marketing message will be "Share all that Curtis offers with your friends."

Sources
Word-of-mouth marketing (referrals by friends) is the most trusted way of trying of getting information about a product or service you are considering trying (www.coolbusinessideas.com, July 2009). Public libraries have very loyal users. Why not see if they would be willing to refer friends and bring them to the library to get a library card?

Value to the library
Will bring in a substantial number of new users to the library. Estimated number of potential new card holders (based on number of new cards from Kindergarten Screening program) = 200

Cost
The costs associated with the program would be minimal:

- E-mail mailing to current library users — No cost
- Press release to local news sources — No cost
- Posters for inside/outside library — $100 (paper and ink)
- Bookmarks for new cardholders — $50
- Buttons—"I got a library card today" — $50
- Extra shift for staff member at lending services — $60
- Tours of the library for new users — No cost except staff time

TOTAL COST — $260

Timeline
- December 15 — Meet with all staff involved, clarify roles and responsibilities
- January 2–9 — Develop marketing program and materials
- January 11–15 — Produce marketing materials in-house
- January 15 — Send out press releases, and e-mail reminders, and distribute marketing materials
- January 22 — Refer a Friend Day

Resources
- Library docents   Provide tours of library on day of event
- Lending services   Extra staff member to register new cardholders
- Mike H.   Develop marketing materials
- Carol I.   Write press releases

Potential issues

A potential issue is that so many people bring in friends for library cards that the Lending Services desk could get swamped. To address this, an additional staff person will be added to the busiest times of the day, and two other librarians will be "on call" if needed to help deal with any overflow.

Success measurement
- 50 new library card registrations (at a minimum)
- Increase library attendance by 20 percent for the day of the event (compared to daily averages for that quarter)

this idea will cost one hundred dollars or one hundred thousand dollars.

- *Timeline:* How long do you think it would take to implement this idea?
- *Resources:* Who would need to be involved in implementing this idea to make it work?
- *Potential issues*: Identify any major issues to consider that might arise as part of this project implementation.
- *Success measurement*: Identify how you will measure success in this project.

That's it. Don't do any more work than what is identified above. What you are doing here is compiling the most essential points for decision makers so they have the information they need to review an idea and decide whether it has merit. You don't want to spend too much time on this, because they could easily come back to you and say no. Your goal is to demonstrate that you have thought through the implications of pursuing this idea, both positive (the value to your library) and negative (cost and resources). Give your proposal to your manager and wait to get a response.

Outcome A: *Approval!* Your project is approved. The next step is to start putting together the team that will execute the project. You should also work with

Table 2
Example of Program Budget

INCOME	BUDGET	ACTUAL
Friends of the Library	$200	$200
Library board discretionary fund	$60	$60
TOTAL Income	$260	$260
EXPENSES		
Posters	$100	$78
Bookmarks	$50	$50
Buttons	$50	$22
Extra staff at lending services	$60	$90
TOTAL Expenses	$260	$240

your manager to ensure that any funding needed for the project is in place and that you will be able to pay for expenses as they come up. To that end, you should develop a simple project budget so that from the first day you are managing your costs. (See table 2.)

Outcome B: *Turned down!* Don't despair. Many good ideas take time to be realized. When an idea is turned down, the first step is to ask for feedback. Here are some questions to ask:

- *Was the idea turned down because it was not a good idea or was not of value to the library?* If so, next time you submit an idea you will know that it is important to make a very strong statement of value.
- *Was the idea turned down because of financial constraints?* Consider whether there is any way to execute the idea less expensively. If not, can you simplify the idea so it will cost less?
- *Was the idea turned down because it used up too much in the way of resources?* If so, consider whether you could have more of the project managed or executed by library volunteers versus paid staff.

- *Was the idea turned down because the decision maker didn't understand the concept?* If so, then you need to clarify the concept and make sure that it can be understood quickly and easily. Consider reading your concept summary to friends and coworkers. Do they understand immediately? If not, then keep reworking the idea.

Above all, if you feel passionately about an idea, don't give up on it at the first rejection. Sometimes it just takes time to clarify a concept or to build support. Keep at it and don't be afraid of rejection. The best ideas will eventually find an audience to support them.

FIFTEEN | # FACILITIES MANAGEMENT

by Robert E. Dugan, director at Mildred Sawyer Library,
Suffolk University, Boston

WHAT THIS CHAPTER IS ABOUT

This chapter will briefly identify and discuss some of the issues concerning the library facility for which a professional librarian with some responsibilities should be aware. Additional details underlying a more complete understanding of facilities will come with experience.

WHY SHOULD YOU CARE?

The facility is a major component of a library's infrastructure, and good library service is facilitated by an efficiently functioning and comfortable physical facility. Many librarians are initially surprised when they first assume some direct responsibilities concerning the physical library building. They have been inside numerous libraries over the years but may not have thought much about the complexities concerning building management, and few courses in graduate library science programs go into the topic in depth. Fortunately, learning about physical facilities does not require an accompanying degree in rocket science.

THE HEART OF THE MATTER
Basics: Understanding What You Have

The general interior layout of the library, including the entrance, the place-ment of its public desks, the stacks, user seating, and programming areas, is one of the first impressions one has of the facility. A question always arises: does the layout follow use, or is use dictated by the layout? One will soon learn that there is a rationale for the layout and how the facility is used. However, as users' needs change, such as the expectation that the library will have an adequate number of publicly accessible computers, the layout may need to be altered to accommodate change. As a result, flexibility in layout—the ability to relocate tables and chairs, and even stacks—is an important facility issue. The less flexible the space, the less adaptable the layout will be to the inevitable changes libraries and the services they offer continuously undertake.

Flexible Furnishings

Furnishings and decor help to accent and emphasize the library's layout. While all furnishings are important, style and color can date a library, and its physical condition can add to a feeling of either "warmth" or "worn." Orange carpeting and beanbag chairs may be retro, but users may think the '60s rather than the twenty-first century. Fortunately, walls can be repainted (maybe a neutral color with a splash of another color for accent) and fabrics updated, which are more cost-effective than replacing the chair or lounge's structure. Carpet tile in two-foot squares is now as cost-affordable as pile car-pets; it is easier to replace one or two damaged tiles than having to replace a larger area of wall-to-wall carpet. Walk-off areas near entrances should have different flooring than in the stacks, and heavy traffic areas (e.g., in front of public desks; to/from one area to another) may be differentiated by differ-ing styles, colors, and textures/fabrics that will hold up well to heavy wear.

A Weighty Matter

One of the infrastructure components of all libraries is its collections. Although digital copies of resources are increasing, most libraries still have shelves of books. The important facility issues concerning stacks are the floor load, stacks height, and aisle width.

Floor load is important because books weigh more than most office and residential furniture and equipment. If your library is located in an older building, understanding floor loads is important to ensure that you aren't overtaxing your building's ability to carry shelving. A single-sided shelving unit of books that is ninety feet high with seven shelves averages one hundred and fifty pounds of weight per square foot. A shelving unit with six shelves (seventy-eight inches high) reduces the weight per square foot to one hundred and twenty-five pounds. Usually, floors supporting books stacks are reinforced to sustain this weight over long distances: for instance, a bookshelf is usually three feet long; a stack may include a dozen or more three-foot-long, seven-shelf vertical units; therefore, the floor may need to sustain one hundred and fifty pounds per square foot over thirty-six or more feet.

Microforms are even heavier per square foot. There are weight differences based upon the format—microfiche versus microfilm—and by the height of the cabinet (number of drawers). A fully loaded, eleven-drawer microfiche cabinet can weigh three hundred pounds per square foot.

Although ninety-foot-high shelving with seven shelves is typical for book collections for adults, one must think also of the user. The top shelf of a seven-shelf unit may be too high for easy reach by some adults and children.

Check Your Accessibility

In addition to height and weight, consider that the stacks must be laid out to comply with aisle widths that meet handicapped accessibility requirements. The minimum aisle width for this is thirty-six inches, although forty-two inches is preferred for ease of access.

In the past three decades, libraries have become aware of and addressed multiple accessibility issues. Responsibility does not end with ensuring that the entrance into the library building is accessible. In some cases with older buildings, the stairs leading to the exterior entrance of the library situates the visitors in a foyer, and a second set of stairs takes one from the foyer to the internal entrance into the library. If there are two such staircases, the library may need to create a separate accessible entrance from the ground level onto the main floor of the library with either an elevator or chairlift to transport the visitor up both levels. It then becomes important to understand how a person moves through the library. It may be that there are levels or specific areas within the library that are inaccessible and can be addressed only with a new building. Too, the public bathrooms are an obvious issue. However, do not forget the furniture and public desks. Is the height of the public desks an obstacle to someone in a wheelchair? Are tables and public computer equipment accessible?

Foot-Candles and Other Lighting Matters

There are various needs for lighting throughout a library, from staff work areas through the stacks, user reading areas, and programming areas. Lighting is generally measured in foot-candles, which are the intensity of light on a surface such as a wall, floor, shelf, table, or chair. The level of light is influenced by many factors such as the availability of natural lighting from the outside (sun through windows or a skylight, filtered or unfiltered) and artificial light from a variety of fixtures and bulbs. Artificial light can also be direct (the light shines directly on the surface) or indirect (it bounces; this is accomplished by directing the path of the light so that it bounces off a wall or ceiling).

The number of foot-candles throughout a library usually varies from one area to another as lighting needs change based upon the area's function as well as the source of the light (direct or indirect artificial light). For most libraries, the range of foot-candles is from thirty to one hundred. However, here's the point: is the lighting in the area comfortable for the function undertaken by either the staff or the users? Is there too much light, too little light, or do staff or users characterize it as harsh or glaring? It may be that the foot-candles can be reduced to ease the uncomfortable lighting, or that an area with all direct lighting be replaced with a mixture of direct and indirect light.

Here is a rule to live by, if possible: enable and provide as much natural light as possible. The layout of the library can be used to emphasize natural light. Instead of putting the book stacks near windows, move the stacks into the interior of the library and place seating along the windows. People like natural light. Install user-controlled blinds so that they may alter the natural light to reduce glare as needed. (Remember, we revolve around the sun and it is in the same place at the same time only once a year.) Too, do not forget the staff. Providing access to natural light for staff members in their work areas will not only help with work productivity, it will also help with morale. Store supplies in a windowless closet, not people.

Temperature, Humidity, and Ventilation

Another basic issue concerns building temperature. Maintenance professionals and architects refer to this as HVAC: heating, ventilation, and air conditioning. HVAC, along with humidity, is a very complex topic, and there are specialists who handle only HVAC building issues. A basic understanding of HVAC and humidity is important, though, for those responsible for monitoring the library—and this generally includes librarians.

Sources of heat/cooling include ceiling-mounted units as well as floor- or wall-mounted units. (A common one is a fan coil unit.) Air ducts in the ceiling, walls, or floors are often used to transport and inject the heated or cooled air from its source into its assigned area. Most often, the temperature in these areas is controlled with thermostats. Air temperatures need to be comfortable to people; this is usually between sixty-five and seventy degrees, although it may be between sixty-eight and seventy-two. That sounds easy enough. However, temperature influences, and is influenced by, relative humidity. Relative humidity is a ratio of the amount of water in the air compared with the amount of water the air can hold at the temperature it happens to be. In a library, a high relative humidity of 60 percent can cause mold to grow; if the relative humidity is below 30 percent, glue used in bookbindings may dry out, resulting in a book losing it pages. Also, a low relative humidity may cause wood to shrink, which can directly affect wooden doors, windows, and bookshelves. Too high a relative humidity causes wood to expand, the result being doors and windows that "stick" and become more difficult to open or close. People feel relative humidity as well as temperature. Libraries should try to maintain a consistent relative humidity at between 40 and 50 percent.

The third part of HVAC is ventilation. Librarians want to make sure that the air within the building is circulating to avoid becoming "stale." Air rotation is usually measured as cubic feet of fresh air per minute, or CFM. The objective is to have the air within each area exchanged. In staff and user areas, that rotation could be as low as three and as high as eight times an hour. Additionally, one wants the air exchanged more often in bathrooms, maybe as high as ten to twelve times per hour.

The Wired Library

Electrical and network wiring is more important now than it was only a decade ago. Staff members depend upon electricity for computers, which also need to be connected through specific network wire to internal and wide area networks (WANs) so as to connect to external resources and eventually the Internet. Too, visitors are using their own personal devices in the library, which require additional access to electrical plugs as well as the wireless network or wired network jacks. Note that even if a wireless network is installed and available in the library, the wireless access point/router must use a network wire to connect to a WAN and an electrical plug (unless powered over Ethernet) to power this network device.

The Exterior of the Building

Let's move outside of the library for a brief look at the building exterior and grounds. The good news is that, in many cases, while the librarian has to know some of the operational and maintenance basics concerning the inside of the library (because that is where the users and staff are most of the time, along with the collections, technology, and library services), the exterior of the building and the grounds are more often the responsibility of the library's institutional parent—the municipal or county government. Regardless of whose responsibility the building and grounds are, the librarian should be thinking: does it require high maintenance or low maintenance?

External building issues concern the construction materials, its appearance, and its upkeep. Identify the building material used—brick or stone, or maybe wood or vinyl siding—and determine its physical condition. Do the bricks or stone look loose, is the paint peeling, or are there any broken windowpanes? Understanding the particulars about the structure's roof is also important. Is the roof sloped or flat? If sloped, what is the material covering the roof (shingles, tiles, or slate are most common)? A flat roof is not uncommon, but its lack of visibility from the ground may hide problems visible on a sloped roof. Also, look at the gutters and downspouts (if any) to determine their condition. Ensure there is clearance on the ground for the downspout to drain properly so water will not back up vertically, which could cause gutter or roof damage.

Another exterior issue to review is the landscaping. The library may be fronted by trees or landscaped with bushes. Are these maintained and trimmed? It is never wise to have any part of a tree or bush touching the exterior of the building. Are the leaves raked? Does the building have curb appeal, and if not, is this something that can be addressed by removing or planting additional bushes or trees?

If the building is fronted by a sidewalk, the walkway should be in good shape; the brick, concrete, or asphalt is not cracked or has no evident heaves caused by frost or tree roots. Please note that it is considerably more difficult to remove snow and ice from brick than it is from an asphalt or concrete sidewalk.

Ideally, the library has, or at least shares, a parking lot. While parking lots may be unnecessary for those libraries served by mass transit, the availability of adequate parking is often a key issue to facilitate and encourage use of the library. The parking lot should have adequate signage from the street so that people can find it. There should be clearly marked lines delineating parking spaces so that as many cars as possible fit onto the lot. Additionally, the parking lot should be well lit for safety after dark. And there should be clearly signed and marked spaces for handicapped parking, appropriately close to the library's handicapped entrance. The parking lot should drain well to eliminate long-standing puddles, which will damage the surface.

Once visitors exit their parked car, it should be obvious to them as to how to proceed to the library. A path should be visible or signage should help direct them. The walkway should take the visitor directly to the main entrance of the library. Additionally, the handicapped entrance should be clearly marked and the plate used to operate the power-assisted door used for wheelchair access clearly visible.

A Few More Basics

We have briefly reviewed the visible interior and exterior of the library building, as well as the grounds. However, there are a couple of other basic issues for a librarian to be aware of.

First is building security. In addition to the book theft detection system installed in many libraries, security is also supported by lighting and cameras. The exterior doors of the library should be well lit. Interior doors should also be lighted differently if possible to emphasize their presence. Installing and using security cameras inside and outside of the library is no longer rare. However, design philosophy comes into play here. Some libraries want the security cameras to be visible and obvious; others prefer that they not attract attention. If possible, libraries should consult with local law enforcement agencies to design, install, and use security systems appropriately.

Another basic and very technical need is to understand local, state, and federal building codes. Dozens if not hundreds of building codes exist covering a wide range of issues, including:

- accessibility to and inside the building
- fire codes, including
  - smoke detectors and alarms
  - sprinkler systems
  - emergency lights and lighting system
  - the height and width of stairwells

- the number of exits
- exit doors and door crash bars, and magnetic door locks which disengage in case of emergency
- signage indicating the paths to the exits
- A rule of thumb: follow the signage. If the signage leads you to a door that will open in an emergency, fine. If, however, you cannot find your way safely out by following the signage, that is a problem.
- carbon dioxide detectors and alarms

- the storage of hazardous materials
- the number of parking spaces
- the number of bathrooms available for the public

Local fire and police departments can be quite helpful in identifying those building codes with which a librarian should be familiar.

Another basic issue concerns the funding allocated or otherwise available for maintaining or updating the facility. This funding may be included in the library's annual operating budget, or may be requested when needed from the local government. Funding may include operational funds, capital project allocations, or bonds to fund construction/maintenance projects for paying back over a long period of time.

Something Can Go Wrong?

Anything can break or go wrong in a library building. Some of the more common maintenance occurrences include lights burning out; electrical fuses failing from electrical jack overloads; wide temperature swings; mold; toilets backing up; water overflowing sinks; spills damaging carpets; doors or windows sticking; paint peeling from walls and woodwork; and leaky roofs and broken windows.

A rule of thumb is that everything needs maintenance at some time. All of the aforementioned maintenance issues can be repaired. However, it is better if the library undertakes preventative maintenance when possible, based upon a plan and schedule. You can develop a "to-do" list to check on mechanical issues that, if unmonitored, can later cause a problem. For example, a dehumidifier should be checked weekly to ensure that its pumps are working, and that the condensed water is not remaining in its spill pan to later overflow onto a floor or ceiling (depending upon the unit's location) because it is not being pumped out.

In some cases, maintenance will be deferred. Although it is known and understood that the maintenance is needed, it is deferred until later because of a lack of money, time, or the availability of skilled workers. It is important that the librarian learn what is being deferred; it is also good practice to keep track of deferred maintenance, to appropriately remind those responsible for the maintenance that it has not been undertaken, and to point out what the consequences of the deferral may be. Such a facilities management issue must be balanced and professionally handled; it must be accomplished without the librarian making threats or overdramatizing the consequences.

Improving the Facility

In addition to understanding as much about the facility as possible while keeping track of its maintenance issues, librarians should always seek ways to improve the facility and thereby improve services and productivity.

A time-proven way is to observe and listen to the library's visitors and staff. What are they asking for? Are they rearranging the furniture, and if so, why? An example may help illustrate this point. When walking the library before opening, you note that some chairs and tables were displaced by users. You put them back into their usual place. A few days later, you notice that the users have moved them again. You again move them back into place. It happens a third time. Why are they moving the furniture? Move the furniture back to its original place, and try to talk to whoever is moving it as to why. It may be that the light is too harsh or weak, or that the furniture is being moved away from a foot traffic area, or it is being moved closer to needed electrical jacks. Internal movement of furniture by users indicates new or changing patterns of library use.

The requests may be for simple needs. Installing a coat rack for the public will ease users' movement around the library. Staff may suggest a centralized light switch replacing all of the switches installed in the public areas, so that less time is spent walking throughout the building flipping light switches before opening and when closing. Additionally, a twenty-first-century library can probably never have enough electrical jacks.

Conclusion

There are a couple of activities a librarian can undertake in order to learn about the physical facility and to keep up with the responsibilities for its management and care. First, become familiar with every square foot by walking it as often as possible, such as once a day before opening. Look at the library layout, and try to determine if the visitors are moving things to better meet their needs. Note burned-out lights and anything else broken, and look for water leaks. Note unwanted variances in temperature or humidity—this may be a harbinger of things to come. Also, listen to the building; a new or different noise or vibration in the building may be an indication of a developing unseen problem. Learn about the age and condition of the building's infrastructure, including the HVAC system, electrical and plumbing systems, and windows, doors, and floor coverings. And do not forget the outside of the building—the roof, gutter system, walls, pathways, and exterior entrances.

Second, create maintenance plans and schedules. For example, it is important to maintain an inventory of furnishings including all seats, tables, wall hangings, lamps, etc., and their acquisition date. The inventory should be reviewed at least annually to quantify loss and can also be useful for creating a furnishings replacement plan. Such a plan may not be executed on schedule, but you will at least know how old everything is and will be able to quickly get into the queue if funds for replacement suddenly become available. Also, create and maintain a wish list of improvement projects and prioritize each relevant to the others.

Even if you do not know the difference between a fan coil unit and light ballast, learn about facilities maintenance. As stated before, it is not rocket science. Ask those knowledgeable, starting with those responsible for maintaining buildings such as the municipal or county facilities crews. They may think you're silly for wanting to learn, but eventually they will come to respect and appreciate your understanding of the facility. In fact, you are becoming their eyes and ears in the building and helping them with their responsibilities. Other helpful municipal or county workers are building inspectors of all types (e.g., structural, electrical, HVAC), planners, and assessors. You may be lucky enough to have a licensed architect or building contractor on one of your library committees who will be able to help.

Another great source of help is other librarians. We are one of the most sharing professions on the planet. We will answer phone calls, visit other libraries, offer advice, and conduct informative and practical presentations and workshops. There are dozens of books concerning buildings and grounds written by peers and published by professional library associations. The state library administrative agency—the government agency found in every state responsible for providing technical assistance to libraries at the local level—likely has one or more staff members with facilities knowledge. They will come to you and share not only their knowledge and experience, but their enthusiasm and passion for library buildings.

In addition to the profession-based books and articles are thousands of websites with information concerning facilities. Want to learn about the formula for a foot-candle? Use a search engine and apply your skills at evaluating the sources and authority of information found on the Internet. The great news about these sources is that they are often free and include illustrations.

Remember that the library is there for the users. As is feasible and practical, involve users in the library and its planning. At the very least, watch how they use the library and listen to their compliments, complaints, and needs concerning the library building, furnishings, and layout. Their perspective is different from yours, and just as important.

SIXTEEN | FIGURES AND FINANCES

WHAT THIS CHAPTER IS ABOUT

Defining how figures and finances will be part of your life as a librarian, identifying some of the basic methods of quantification and measurement that you will work with, and providing simple ways of managing that information without fear

WHY SHOULD YOU CARE?

Data. You hate working with numbers, but you can't live without the information they provide. Measurement and standards are an integral part of every librarian's life today because they are how you track your resources, and they give you an objective form of evaluation for spending that you can then use to rationalize why your library should receive continued financial support. In today's world you need to demonstrate that what you do has value, and quantification is the best way to do that.

THE HEART OF THE MATTER

If you are like the majority of librarians, you don't like numbers, you aren't particularly intrigued by statistics, you see data as the Great Satan, and your sincere hope was that by becoming a librarian you would never have to see another number in your life. In the past, that might have been a possibility. Sadly for those of us who are number-phobes, data is an important part of our jobs as librarians today. The objective of this chapter isn't to teach you to love budgeting, numbers, statistics, data, and other quantified information, but rather to demonstrate how to use them effectively and accurately when necessary in your job, and to help you lose your fear and avoidance. The following are my basic "facts and figures for librarians" tools.

Tool 1: *Learn how to use Microsoft Excel.* There is no way around this one. You have to at least be able to find your way around a spreadsheet, even if you don't become an expert at it. You will use Excel to track the number of people who use your library, to track book buying, to track spending on book buying, to track the number of interlibrary loans . . . the list goes on and on. If you don't feel your Excel skills are adequate, ask to take a class as soon as you start your new job. If there is no funding for staff development, see if your state library association provides access to WebJunction, an online learning site for librarians where you will be able to take basic classes in Excel. If that doesn't work, check *Excel for Dummies* out of the library and practice on your own. There are also several online resources that provide basic classes in Excel. These classes are a good way of learning Excel, because they allow you to move at your own speed. Bottom line: find a way to learn how to manage a basic spreadsheet, so that when someone in your library asks you to track the circulation of mystery books over a period of six months, you have a simple, effective way of doing that.

Tool 2: *Learn how to calculate "percentage difference."* One of the measures most frequently tracked by libraries (of all types) is the percentage increase or decrease from one period to another (month to month, year to year, week to week) in library traffic, library lending, spending, etc. It is a very simple calculation and if you can learn it right here and now, you will be happy you did. This example will look at how to track the increase or decrease in lending volume between 2007 and 2008.

Lending volume for 2008
- lending volume for 2007
÷ by lending volume 2007
= percentage change in lending volume between 2008 and 2007

100,000 - 90,000 = 10,000 ÷ 90,000 = +11.1%

There are a few things to remember about this calculation:

- It works for any measure to be evaluated: volume, number of patrons, dollars spent, etc.
- You are trying to determine how much increase or decrease there has been in a specific measurement over a period of time. So always start with the most recent time period measurement and subtract from that the starting time period (2008 minus 2007). You might get a negative number if the number decreased between the first and second period. Divide the resulting number by the starting time period (in this case 2007).

This isn't a difficult calculation, but it is a very important one that you should be able to do quickly. You'll find that if you are comfortable with this calculation, it will become one of the most used tools that you will employ in your job.

Tool 3: *Measurements of use.* Libraries vary tremendously in the degree to which they track and evaluate their performance. The following list identifies some of the most basic measures that every library should track. Upon starting a new position, you might want to ask to see your library's performance measurements and, if they do not exist, offer to track them yourself. Nothing

Additional Examples of Calculating Percentage Change

In 2008 your library spent $1,120,000 on materials. In 2007 the library spent $1,700,000. How much did the budget change from year to year?
Answer: 1,120,000 - 1,700,000 = -580,000 ÷ 1,700,000 = -34.1%

In January your library circulated 47,000 items. In February your library circulated 53,400 items. How much did circulation change?
Answer: 53,400 - 47,000 = 6,400 ÷ 47,000 = +13.6%

speaks more loudly about the positive value of what a library provides to its community than clear and definitive numbers.

How many people walk through your door every month and every year? The best way to collect this information is to have an electronic counter on all doors into your building and track the numbers on a weekly basis. If your library can't afford to purchase an electronic counter, then the next best step is to have a staff member count the number of people that walk through the library doors for busy, moderate, and slow times of the day and extrapolate a number for the year. The average number of visitors to your library is a critical measurement tool to have. It tells your funding authorities the extent to which the community is using the library and, as you track the number from year to year, if that usage is increasing or decreasing.

Here is an example of how to do this:

- Identify a slow, average, and very busy hour in your library.
- During each of those three time periods, count the number of visitors coming into your library.
- Find the average of those three numbers. For example, 20 during a slow period, 40 during an average period, 75 during a busy period. In this case, the average would be 45 people per hour.
- Multiple that number times the number of hours you are open each week (45 people times 50 hours per week = 2,250 people through the library doors per week). Now, multiply by the number of weeks you are open in a year and you have an average number of visitors per year (2,250 people x 52 weeks = 117,000 people per year).
- Of course this number isn't exact, but it does give you a rough estimate of the number of visitors to your library per year. What is most important is to keep your calculation consistent from year to year. This means to get your average visitors by evaluating the same time periods in the same months every year. This will allow you to understand if your average usage is going up or down.

How many materials are circulated at your library? Circulation measurements are tricky. They are only useful as a tool of measurement in comparison to something else. For example, if you tell someone that your library circulated one hundred thousand books last year, there is no way to understand if that number is good, bad, or indifferent because there is nothing to which to compare it. However, if you say that the number of books circulated at your library has increased 50 percent every year for each of the past five years, then you can understand that this library's circulation is growing at a good rate. Or, if your library's circulation is one hundred thousand and all other similar-sized libraries in your state circulate approximately fifty thousand items, then you know your library is being well used, because you have a point of comparison.

Tracking circulation is something that every library does, whether by hand or via a computerized system. However, not all libraries define key points of comparison for their circulation. Some ideas for doing this include picking two to three other libraries in your state or system that are of roughly the same size and comparing your library's circulation to theirs; tracking your library's circulation over six-month periods and comparing them to the same periods in prior years to understand if your usage is trending up or down; and tracking your circulation in particular after you've done a specific program at your library to see if the number of items increases as a direct result of the program execution.

How many programs and number of attendees at programs? This measurement of use is simple. You count the number of attendees at programs and the number of programs each month at your library. This number is much like the circulation number—it doesn't mean much except in comparison to something else. So you might want to compare the number of attendees to a program this year, versus the number of attendees to the same program last year. Or you might evaluate the total number of programs at your library this year versus last year. What caused the increases or declines? Again, the number itself isn't as important as the comparison that you do with it.

How many reference questions do we field? When we track reference questions, we divide them into two types of questions: real reference questions ("I need a medical resource so I can understand the impact of diabetes on my spouse") versus what we call "directional" reference questions ("Where is the bathroom?" or "Where do I find this book?"). It helps to know if there is a specific time of the year when library users ask more reference questions (you might get more medical reference questions in midwinter, when people tend to get sick more) to meet staffing needs at the reference desk. It is also helpful to track the number of question from year to year to see how effective a reference department is in maintaining its relevance to an increasingly Internet-oriented customer.

How many cardholders do we have? At public libraries the number of cardholders is a critical measurement of use. Library funding groups expect the number of cardholders to increase or at least stay even from year to year. If this doesn't happen, then you need to understand why.

How much money do we spend on the library collection? The amount of money spent on your collection is a measurement of the health of your library. By itself, the amount doesn't tell you anything. However, if you compare your spending with other, similar libraries and find that you are spending far less (or in some rare instances, far more), then you need to understand why. It also provides a compelling piece of data to be able to go to your funding authorities and demonstrate with data how your library's spending doesn't "measure up" to your competitors.

Tool 4: *Learn the basics of your library's budget.* If your first job as a new librarian is in a large library, it is unlikely that you will have to see or worry about the library's budget. However, if your first job is in a small library, it is very likely that you will be involved with the yearly budget development in some capacity, and in fact you may end up having to manage the budget yourself. In any case, it is always helpful to a library director to have staff members who understand how a budget is put together and managed, so it is never a bad thing to gain a basic understanding of budgeting.

At its simplest level, a budget defines what expenses in a library will require funding over a fiscal year. At a more theoretical level, a budget defines the expectations of an organization from a financial perspective. Most libraries are nonprofit organizations of one type or another, so their budgets generally balance out income and expenses to zero. However, their status as nonprofits does not make a budget any less important to them. It is still critical to have a budget so that expectations are established as to how spending will occur throughout a fiscal year. Clear definition of anticipated spending patterns will ensure that all those involved in running a library are in agreement as to how money will be spent.

A budget is established before the beginning of a fiscal year. (A fiscal year is the defined period of time, most often July 1 through June 30, during which budgets are managed.) A library's yearly operating budget defines how much money will be needed by a library to keep the doors open, the lights on, and staffing in place over the course of a year. The operating budget will generally identify fixed and variable costs. *Fixed costs* are any expenses that are the same regardless of use. An example might be what your library pays for interlibrary loan delivery. If the cost is the same regardless of how often you use the delivery service, then it is a fixed cost. If the cost changes depending on how often you use the service, then it is a *variable cost.* Utility costs are another example of variable costs. They change depending on how much electricity or oil or gas your building uses.

During the course of a fiscal year, spending may match the budget expectations or expenses may fluctuate depending on what is going on in the library. Your budget does not change in accordance with those fluctuations.

(Remember: once established, a budget never changes.) What changes is your *budget update*. Libraries do budget updates over different periods of time. In my library I see weekly budget updates, but I generally share that information with the library's board of directors once a month. Budget updates help you understand if your spending is on track against the expectations defined in the budget.

A budget and the budget updates can be laid out in many different ways. The basic format for an operating budget is to identify first your income and then your expenses. Each of your expenses will fall into a specific category of expense such as "personnel expenses." These would cover anything to do with library staffing, such as salaries or benefits. The category of expense is called a *line item*.

Some libraries have the flexibility to manage their operating budgets more aggressively than others. One library may be able to manage the budget at the *bottom line*. This means that at the end of the year, the library director is only responsible for ensuring that the library does not overspend its total budget. In this situation the director has the option of moving money between line items, depending on changing priorities. In other libraries, there may be rules that funds can be moved only within a line item. In that situation, a director might be able to move money within the personnel line item from salaries to staff development. However, the director cannot move money from personnel to equipment purchasing. One type of budget management is not better or worse than the other. They simply indicate different levels of control.

The more time you spend looking at and reviewing budgets and budget updates, the more comfortable you'll be with the process of budgeting. If you would like experience with budgets, ask your manager if you can establish a budget for a program that you are developing. The principle of budgeting is the same for a program or for the library's operating budget. By managing a budget at a project level, you'll get a good understanding of how your library's operating budget is managed at a larger level.

Tool 5: *Understand a profit and loss statement.* A profit and loss (P&L) statement is exactly what it sounds like. It defines how much revenue is expected by an organization over the course of a year and how many expenses will be incurred to drive that revenue. The net result of income minus expenses will result in the operating profit of the organization. A P&L is used to evaluate the day-to-day or immediate operations of the library. It does not consider the *capital expenses* of the library. Capital items can be thought of as anything that will affect the library across multiple years. A good example of a capital item is the library building or the library collection. See the discussion below under tool 6 for further discussion about capital items. Profit and loss statements are typically generated monthly throughout a fiscal year so an organization can see how it is progressing against its goals for achieving profit. If an organization is not achieving its goals, an organizational manager can *manage* their P&L to try to reach its goals. Managing a P&L means that the manager may try to increase revenue or cut expenses to reach the desired profit level. Generally, as long as a library balances out revenue and expenses, it has met its goals. Because most libraries are nonprofit organizations, they frequently do not concern themselves with a profit and loss statement. However, it is still a useful concept to understand, since some libraries do use P&Ls as a way of evaluating their performance over the course of a year.

Tool 6: *Learn to read a balance sheet.* A P&L defines the yearly or short-term financial expectations of where a library will get revenue and where it will spend money. In comparison, a balance sheet is a one-time snapshot of an organization's complete financial situation. It includes any money in bank accounts or in the library's endowment. It includes property owned by the library. A balance sheet defines the overall health (or illness) of an institution by putting all of its financial assets (positive cash flow) and liabilities (negative cash flow) in one place. A balance sheet is really an accounting tool in that it provides information—but it is not information that you would or could generally act upon (unless you plan to sell your library building!). A balance sheet is important, because it helps keep track if you are dipping into long-term savings for short-term benefit. For example, you might look at a balance sheet and see that your library's checking account for day-to-day operational expenses has been tapped out. That means that you might have to transfer funds from your library's endowment to cover the shortage in cash in your checking account. Essentially, you are taking money from long-term savings and putting those funds against a short-term expense. This may be a necessity, but it also indicates the need for a strategic discussion with your library governing body. A balance sheet is useful for identifying issues of this type and provoking discussion.

OTHER RESOURCES

The Motley Fool. www.fool.com.
> Has a good description of how to read a balance sheet at www.fool.com/investing/beginning/how-to-value-stocks-how-to-read-a-balance-sheet.aspx. Motley Fool is also a good site for general financial how-to advice.

Richards, P. J. "How to Read a Profit and Loss Statement." www.ehow.com/
how_2306963_read-profit-loss-statement.html.
A simple description of a profit and loss statement and how to read it. Very
helpful for the beginner at business math

Sterling, Mary Jane. *Business Math for Dummies.* Hoboken, NJ: Wiley, 2008.
There are several books similar to this one on the market. It isn't a book
to sit down and read through from front to back. However, if you are
uncomfortable with math and finance, it is a great resource to have on hand
when you need to do some figurin'.

INDEX

Page numbers in italic refer to information in shaded boxes.

emotions, management of, *65,* 66
end-of-aisle spaces, use of, 96–97
environment of library, 9
evaluation of team efforts, 81
events, promotion of, 89
Excel, use of, 134
expenses, personal, *4*
    See also budgeting, personal
exterior of building, 126–127
eye-level placement, 95–96

F
facilities management, 121–131
    accessibility, 123–124, 127
    exterior, 126–127
    furnishings, 96, 122, 124, 129, 130
    HVAC systems, 124–125
    maintenance, 128–129, 130
    shelving, 95–96, 122–123
    wiring, 125–126
fads *vs.* trends, 110
fears, mastering, 70, *73,* 74
feedback from community
    incorporating into your work, 34–35
    on library events, 89–90, *90*
    talking with regular users, 98–99
feedback from manager, 16–18
finances, library, 133–141
finances, personal, 4–5
fiscal year, definition, 138
fixed costs, 138
floor coverings, 122
floor load, 123
follow up with new contacts, *26–27*
foot-candles, 124
friendships and partnering, 25
funding for building maintenance,
    128
furnishings
    accessibility of, 124
    flexibility of, 122
    inventory of, 130
    movement of by users, 129
    and neatness of library, 96

G
Google Docs and teamwork, 81
grocery shopping, *94*
gross pay *vs.* net pay, 5

gut instincts
    about potential coworkers, 10
    as guide for taking a job, 5, 8

H
handicapped accessibility, 123–124, 127
heating in building, 124–125
human resources
    as specialty, *15*
    as support in conflicts with manager,
        64
humidity in building, 125
humor in dealing with problem patrons,
    57–58
HVAC systems, 124–125

I
ideas
    developing, 114, 115
    presenting, 128–129, 130
    responses to new ideas, *41, 43*
ideas, presenting, 80
illustrations in presentations, 74
information literacy. *See* library literacy
    as specialty
Internet, sources for free information
    and training on, 18–19
interviews, 107
inventory of furnishings, 130
    See also furnishings

J
job opportunities
    and elevator pitches, 32
    and partnering, 25
jobs, selection of, 3–13
    comparison of previous jobs with
        current job, *43*
    gut instincts about, 5, 8, 10
    less than perfect, 8
    preferred characteristics of, 9–10
    pressures to take inappropriate jobs,
        3–4
    salary requirements, 4–5, *6–7*
journaling of observations, 41–42

L
landscaping, 126
layout of library, 122

weeding as ongoing process, 97
welcoming place, library as, *94*
wiring of building, 125–126
workplace culture, 39–44
    adjusting to, 42–43, *43*
    observing, 39–42

    poor fit to, 43–44
    See also coworkers
workspace for staff, 9
writing as advocacy, 34

You may also be interested in

Creating Your Library Brand: Communicating Your Relevance and Value to Your Patrons: In this book Doucett covers everything from working with outside experts to evaluating and maintaining your library's brand, illustrated by case studies from several libraries. End-of-chapter exercises enhance the feedback process. Tips, suggestions for success, and answers to frequently asked questions ensure your team collaborates on a library brand that will bring more patrons through the door!

Writing and Publishing: The Librarian's Handbook: If you are interested in writing or reviewing for the library community or in publishing a book, or if you need to write and publish for tenure, then *Writing and Publishing* is for you. This book includes practical how-to guidance covering fiction, poetry, children's books/magazines, self-publishing, literary agents, personal blogging, and other topics.

Developing an Outstanding Core Collection: A Guide for Libraries, Second Edition: In this practical, newly updated handbook, Carol Alabaster focuses on developing a collection with high-quality materials while saving time and money. Packed with selection resources and sample core lists in seven subject areas, this soup-to-nuts manual will be useful whether you are starting from scratch or revitalizing an existing collection.

Fundamentals of Library Supervision, Second Edition: Guiding supervisors through the intricate process of managing others, this comprehensive handbook addresses the fundamental issues facing new managers. It also serves as a welcome refresher and reference for experienced managers facing new challenges in this complex and changing environment.

Order today at www.alastore.ala.org or 866-746-7252!

ALA Store purchases fund advocacy, awareness, and accreditation programs for library professionals worldwide.